DATE DUE

DEMCO 38-296

Fables
Less and Less
Fabulous

Fables
Less and Less
Fabulous

English Fables and Parables
of the Nineteenth Century
and Their Illustrations

Horst Dölvers

DELAWARE

Newark: University of Delaware Press
London: Associated University Presses

© 1997 by Associated University Presses, Inc.

ed University Presses
440 Forsgate Drive
Cranbury, NJ 08512

Associated University Presses
16 Barter Street
London WC1A 2AH, England

Associated University Presses
P.O. Box 338, Port Credit
Mississauga, Ontario
Canada L5G 4L8

The paper used in this publication meets the requirements
of the American National Standard for Permanence of Paper
for Printed Library Materials Z39.48–1984.

Library of Congress Cataloging-in-Publication Data

Dölvers, Horst, 1937–
 Fables less and less fabulous : English fables and parables of the
nineteenth century and their illustrations / Horst Dölvers.
  p. cm.
 Incudes bibliographical references and index.
 ISBN 0-87413-584-2 (alk. paper)
 1. Fables, English—History and criticism. 2. English
literature—19th century—History and criticism. 3. Children's
literature, English—History and criticism. 4. Didactic literature,
English—History and criticism. 5. Illustration of books—19th
century—Great Britain. 6. English literature—19th century—
Illustrations. 7. Didactic literature, English—Illustrations.
8. Parables—History and criticism. 9. Fables, English—
Illustrations. 10. Parables—Illustrations. I. Title.
PR468.F32D64 1997
820.9'008—dc20   96-38210
                                                                CIP

PRINTED IN THE UNITED STATES OF AMERICA

The fabulist now seeks analogies where before he merely sought humorous situations. The machinery ... becomes less and less fabulous.

—Robert Louis Stevenson (1874)

Contents

List of Illustrations

ACKNOWLEDGMENTS

Thanks are due to the following for furnishing photographs and granting permission to reproduce them: the Herzog von Ratibor'sche Generalverwaltung, Corvey, for Northcote's "The Lobsters" (1828); the British Library for Alfred Crowquill's "The Lobsters" (1854) and the Election Broadsheet (1881); the Bayerische Staatsbibliothek, Munich, for the plate from Corrozet's *Hecatomgraphie* (1543); the Staatsbibliothek zu Berlin, Preussischer Kulturbesitz, for Speckter's illustrations from Hey's *Fünfzig Fabeln für Kinder* (1833); and the Victoria and Albert Museum for the Alma Tadema photograph.

Preface

THIS book is a late attempt to make amends for a regrettable omission. When I published a New Critical monograph on Robert Louis Stevenson in 1969, I thought I might as well skip over his fables. No critic had ever set much store by them, and Stevenson himself did not publish them in his lifetime. After all, did fables count for anything in the nineteenth century?

They certainly did, as I found out about two decades later, when, true to the saying, the offender returned to the scene of the offense. For one thing Stevenson's last, elusive texts bear witness to a kind of creative effort entirely different from what he had done in his roughcast romances and his overly demonstrative *Dr. Jekyll and Mr. Hyde.* Of course one always sees what one anticipates. In literary criticism a new interest that reaches beyond irony and ambiguity (as tensions within the text as a unified whole) to an oscillation of meanings that play havoc with the idea of the text itself helped to identify what one might call Stevenson's self-controverting (anti-)fables.

Second, it turned out that Stevenson, late in the nineteenth century, was not a lonely hunter. In a seemingly innocuous picture book with Aesopian fables in limericks (1887), Walter Crane, the artist and illustrator, and his author, William J. Linton, both socialists, had already played wolves in sheep's clothing by subtly undermining what seemed obvious in word and image and making commonsense meanings available for political and gender criticism. More surprisingly Lord Lytton, in two volumes of *Fables in Song* (1874), had likewise put the "ancient Fox of Fable" (as he put it) to rather unfamiliar tasks. As for the lambs, it soon became evident that many authors who now figure in the literary canon (as well as a host of writers who do not) at least once in a while tried their hands at fable writing, often transforming the genre into something new and fascinating. The age simply abounded in fables. And fables, as they evolved in the course of the century from vessels of emblematic truth into rather brittle repositories of skepticism and indecisiveness, can nowadays be seen as mirroring on a small scale a more general loss of security and faith. "'Then,' I said," (to continue with Lytton's words, but meaning fables, the whole lot that soon turned up),

> "whatsoever they be
> That I meet, as the change may come,
> If I speak to, and question them all—. . .
> Will they answer me? Tell me, O tell!
> For, look you, I love them well."
> The Fox, as he turn'd aside,
> Gave me a friendly glance;
> And, fading into the forest, replied
> With encouraging voice, "Perchance.
> Try!" And so . . . Well, I have tried.

Encouragement of a less fabulous kind came from John Dixon Hunt, Erwin Wolff, Dieter Mehl, Bernhard Kettemann, and Walter T. Rix, who published earlier versions of five of the chapters in *Word & Image, Anglia, Archiv für das Studium der neueren Sprachen und Literaturen, Arbeiten aus Anglistik und Amerikanistik,* and *Literatur in Wissenschaft und Unterricht.* Jay L. Halio, the editorial board of the University of Delaware Press, and their anonymous reader were demanding, yet, ultimately, reassuring critics. To them all I am grateful for their confirmation that I had not thrown away my time on a subject of little or no relevance.

To Michael Nerlich and Reinhard Krüger, Berlin, I am obliged for their invitations, years ago, to talk about fables and their illustrations at a symposium *Image et Texte,* hosted by the Institut für Romanische Literaturwissenschaft, Technische Universität Berlin, together with the École des Hautes Études en Sciences Sociales, Paris. They can hardly have anticipated that (as in "The Farmer's Treasure" by Linton/Crane) they sent me digging through a field where "the Treasure was found in the yield." Further thanks are due to Joachim Möller, who, somewhat later, invited me to his delightful symposium on *English Book Illustration in Its European Context.* Most cordially I wish to thank Andrea von Dietrich (who discussed some of the earlier versions with me) for a great number of helpful suggestions and her enthusiastic response to "Kinder sind keine kleinen Erwachsenen." Susanne Rupp has offered valuable criticism and toiled for many hours checking the text and collating the quotations in the British Library. Finally my thanks go to Ian Trotter and Lawrence Harding for their careful reading of parts of the manuscript. But, again with Linton/Crane, "Spare your Benefactors!"[1]

Introduction: The Fable of the Fable's Death

Aт first sight in nineteenth-century Europe the fable, Aesopian or parabolic, would seem to have lost much of its importance. It had flourished in the seventeenth and eighteenth centuries, when La Fontaine's *Fables* came out between 1668 and 1694, Gay's *Fables* appeared in 1727 and 1738, and Lessing published three books of his *Fabeln* in 1759. From the Romantic period onward, however, traditional fables and their modern imitations and variants alike went through a sharp decline in prestige in Germany, France, and England. Around the year 1800, there was already talk among critics of "the death of the fable."[1]

In our days this metaphor has become something of a self-fulfilling obituary. Because they are deemed of no more than marginal importance, nineteenth-century fables are rarely discussed or even mentioned. Literary histories covering that period have completely lost sight of the genre. This is not, in fact, due to a restricted notion of what is "literary," taking into account only texts of a certain complexity and sophistication. Studies focusing on the social context, such as Amy Cruse's compendious works *The Englishman and His Books* (1930) and *The Victorians and Their Books* (1935), treat a broad range of unsophisticated texts, but there is no mention of fables. Books for the general reader on *The Victorian Scene, Victorian People and Ideas,* or even *The Pleasures of the Victorian Age* and *Victorian Entertainment* offer information on the Aesthetic Movement, the Alphabet of Flowers, actors, acrobats, and reenactments of the Afghan War, but not on Aesop. They discuss the Fabians, family prayers, and fairground arts, but not fables—parliament, parodies, pantomimes, and panoramas, but not parables.[2] In Germany, Lothar Hönnighausen's magisterial study of symbolic and allegorical literary forms in the second half of the nineteenth century, *Präraphaeliten und Fin de Siècle* (1971), covers a variety of allegorical-typological texts but does not say a word about fables or parables. Theo Elm, in his book *Die mod-*

erne Parabel, calls the nineteenth century "a period without parables."[3]

The following study has as its subject more than one hundred fables in prose and verse, most of them original in content, some highly original in form. Thus there is strong evidence that the obituary on the fable has been premature and that the story of the fable's demise is itself—if one takes the term in its widest sense—nothing but a fable: "a short tale, obviously false."[4] Probably most students of Victorian literature today will have run into fables in their own areas of research and will regard this reassessment as no more than a truism. It remains to be shown, however, that pushing the fable out of sight has robbed English studies of a subject that may occasionally appear simple but is frequently anything but plain.

It is true that the number of fable collections (at least for adults) fell off sharply at the beginning of the century, and the genre ceased to play an important role in criticism. Thomas Noel, in his *Theories of the Fable in the Eighteenth Century* (1975), has assembled the evidence for some European countries under the heading "dissolution of a functioning literary genre," and he speaks of the "decay" and later of the "demise" of the fable.[5] He considers several possible causes. A new bourgeois readership may have developed a more fastidious taste, while life began to appear more complex. The didactic element in literature lost its importance, and antiquity was, after all, no longer the prevalent model in literature and thought, so that epic and fable together lost much of their standing.

From a broader empirical basis, Stephen H. Daniel (1982) has slightly modified these assumptions. He observes a gradual *assimilation* of the genre to bourgeois sensibility. Thus in one respect, he connects the "decline of the fable form" in its educational and entertaining variants with an increasing delicacy and daintiness in fable collections that presented themselves to the reader as *Sentimental Fables* (1771) or *Fables Moral and Sentimental* (1772). At the same time, he agrees that contemporary discussions of the more "serious" moral, social, political, and philosophical fable writing indicate that the "didactic" ascription of speech and reason to animals increasingly was perceived as detracting from "truth" as well as "good sense," while the traditional animal fable's prudential morality, based on the observation of cunning in animal behavior, would seem to have been in conflict with more profound speculations on man's relationships with the natural world.[6]

Already in 1973 Harald Weinrich had suggested an explanation in the larger context of contemporary *Geistesgeschichte.* He pointed to what has been called a "move toward temporality" *(Verzeitlichung)* in the sciences of the nineteenth century. As a new principle to reduce complexity, temporal categories generally seem to have replaced "the a-temporal moral reduction principle of the fable," and "historical imagination fought with the moral imagination of the fabulists." Thus Aesop, La Fontaine, Gay, and Lessing had to hand over their authority and withdraw, "almost forgotten," into "the marginal zones of philological editions and text books, illustrated children's literature . . . literature in dialect . . . humor and caricature . . . and a few moralist writings."[7]

As it happens, one of these marginal areas has aroused renewed critical interest in Germany over the last two decades: there have been several studies of German children's literature. Contrary to what might be expected, these studies record an increase in the number of fables between 1815 and 1830. Ariane Neuhaus-Koch, for instance (in Peter Hasubek's *Fabelforschung,* 1983), writes about texts by Langbein, Haug, and Fröhlich and points out the degree to which their fables provided "positive patterns of behavior and communication in family, marriage and friendship," contributing to a conformist attitude and the stability of the state. Neuhaus-Koch goes on to give a detailed account of both Grillparzer and Heine (the latter much read at the time in England) and discusses the way in which Heine, who admitted to having "versified a large number of funny animal fables," held their morals in a most delicate and ironical balance.[8] This was very different from what Wilheim Hey did with *his* verse fables (1833, 1837—widely known in England as well with their idyllic illustrations by Otto Speckter), which depicted the child's world as safe, sheltering, and full of moral significance. Hey's fables flooded the market and were frequently reprinted up to the twentieth century. Women writers in particular produced attractive (if sometimes rather smug) variations on Aesopian motifs and combined their talents with highly skilled illustrators like Fedor Flinzer. Wilhelm Busch, poet and artist, remodeled fables into his immortal picture tales which were full of scathing satire—"the genre at its height" (Neuhaus-Koch). What has been regarded as "almost forgotten" seems to have been very much alive and not infrequently kicking.

There is ample evidence that much the same holds true for Great Britain and the United States. But here the prevailing

Otto Speckter, "Murmeltier tanzt" *Reproduced by permission of the Staatsbibliothek Berlin*

impression that fables lost out in the course of the nineteenth century has come under hardly any revision so far. It would seem that Max Plessow's *Geschichte der Fabeldichtung in England* (1906) set a fateful pattern in closing with John Gay. Later monographs on the English fable and its illustrations (e.g., M. E. Smith's "Notes on the Rimed Fable" [1916] or Edward Hodnett's *Aesop in England* [1979]) have likewise restricted their scope to earlier centuries. In Germany, Hermann Lindner's anthology *Fabeln der Neuzeit* (1978) helped to reinforce the impression that at the time of Queen Victoria the English-speaking countries did not give a penny (or a cent) for the fable. Due to "an excessive backlog in research" there is a gap—or rather a chasm—in his collection between Thomas Moore (1823) and James Thurber (1940). H. J. Blackham's study titled *The Fable as Literature* (1985) skips over the whole of the nineteenth century.[9]

Only quite recently have two monographs incorporated nineteenth-century fable material within their much wider scope. In a delightful annotated edition of fable illustrations through the centuries, Anne S. Hobbs, in 1986, gave a cross-

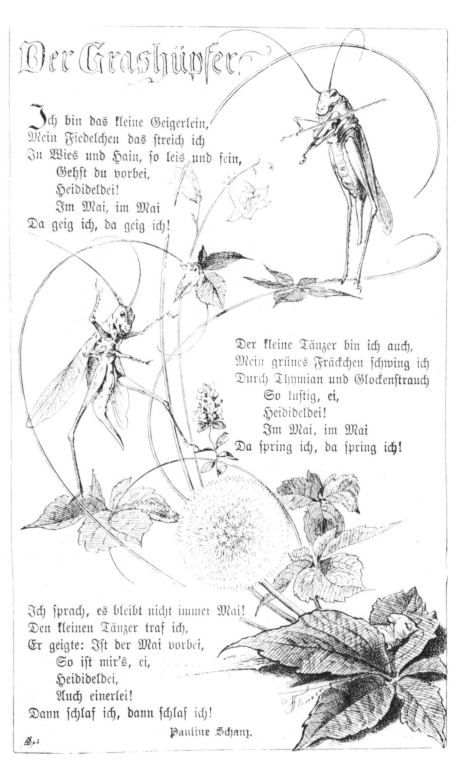

Der Grashüpfer

Ich bin das kleine Geigerlein,
Mein Fiedelchen das streich ich
In Wies und Hain, so leis und fein,
  Gehst du vorbei,
  Heidideldei!
  Im Mai, im Mai
Da geig ich, da geig ich!

Der kleine Tänzer bin ich auch,
Mein grünes Fräckchen schwing ich
Durch Thymian und Glockenstrauch
  So lustig, ei,
  Heidideldei!
  Im Mai, im Mai
Da spring ich, da spring ich!

Ich sprach, es bleibt nicht immer Mai!
Den kleinen Tänzer traf ich,
Er geigte: Ist der Mai vorbei,
  So ist mir's, ei,
  Heidideldei,
  Auch einerlei!
Dann schlaf ich, dann schlaf ich!

Pauline Schanz.

Fedor Flinzer, "Der Grashüpfer"

Und Spitz und Kater fliehn im Lauf. –
Der größte Lump bleibt obenauf!! –

Wilhelm Busch, from "Hans Huckebein"

section of pictures in printed books between Steinhöwel's *Aesop* of 1476 and Felix Hoffmann's designs of 1968, including illustrations by Bewick (1818), Tenniel (1848), Bennett (1857), Weir (1872), Caldecott (1883), and Crane (1887). And Annabel Patterson, in her *Fables of Power: Aesopian Writing and Political History* (1991), though treating extensively only the sixteenth and seventeenth centuries, concluded with remarks on the social and political implications of a satirical fable in verse of 1831, a fable compilation of 1866, and the use of the body-and-its-members metaphor in George Eliot's *Felix Holt, the Radical* (1866) and in Karl Marx's *Value, Price, and Profit* (1865). I will return to the first two of Patterson's instances in chapter 1 when I look into continuities concerning fable compilation, moral and social "application" and satire, and later discuss ideological implications of fable matter extensively in my analyses of a picture book and a best-seller animal romance.

In actual fact, the Fox of Fable was just as alive in England as on the Continent and just as ready to slip into fancy dress. He can be spotted under the ass's hide of satire as easily as under the sheepskin of a child's toy. In *vers de société* and royalty ballads, he hid among leaves and "branches bending down to the ground" or frolicked among bees and butterflies, roses, daffodils, and daisies, which took over plot roles better known from Aesop. At other times, exceedingly earnest, he peeped out from under a preacher's garment or a philosopher's gown.

The use of *personificatio* in the foregoing paragraph has been suggested by a nineteenth-century text. In the Earl of Lytton's *Fables in Song* (1874), we meet the "ancient Fox of Fable" informing the narrator, in a pensive and reproachful tone, of his fate when the times became unfriendly to fable lore. Here, of his many roles, he adopts one more—he plays the nostalgic conservative, a critic of the increasing rationalism and skepticism of the time, holding the mirror up to an age that is cutting itself off from transcendence: "A false Aesop you formed of your own, / We, the children of Aesop, withdrew."[10]

Lytton's *Fables,* which will be extensively studied at a later point, contain many such tales in which a moral or philosophical problem is given an allegorical guise and discussed to some extent. At first sight, this is a far cry from Aesop, and some critics might prefer to exclude texts of this sort from the fable genre altogether and call them either "allegories" (as in William Adams's *Sacred Allegories*), "parables" (as in Margaret Gatty's *Parables from Nature*), or (with one of Lytton's own terms) "reveries." Thus, a short note on terminology is called for.

I shall follow Lord Lytton's example (and recent research) and give the term "fable" an inclusive meaning. The material shows that for the nineteenth century there is little sense in distinguishing between fables and parables along the lines of, say, the fables of Aesop and Lessing's *Ring Parable.* The criteria for separating the two have never been very clear anyway. One might argue that relative shortness, conventional characters, a skeptical rationality, and pragmatic views characterize fables, whereas a greater length and a pleading for more general moral or philosophical positions, or even "higher metaphysical insights and hermeneutic potential," identify parables.[11] But, of course, Swift's famous analogue to Lessing's *Ring Parable* is generally known as "The Fable of the Coats" (1704), which is what Swift called it himself. Bernard Mandeville continued to identify his long, controversial *Fable of the Bees* (1714) in repeated editions as a fable. Conversely biblical "parables" occasionally have the nonhuman agents, the shortness and terseness, and the pragmatic message of the fable—see the parables of Jotham and Joas of how the thorn-bush was anointed king by the trees ("you have made Abimelech, the son of my father's slave-girl, king over the citizens of Shechem") and of how a thistle in Lebanon wooed a cedar ("Stay at home and enjoy your triumph"). Significantly short conventional fables had been employed in theological or religious discussions for decades when John Toland, in 1695, warned that they tended only to confound religious doctrines and to make them all the more mysterious and inaccessible to ordinary man.[12]

More relevantly, in the nineteenth century "seriousness" finally invaded the shorter, more worldly form, so that the distinction broke down once and for all. Fable matter was incorporated into the far more respectable category of Christian typological verse. "Frail is the bond by which we hold / Our being, whether young or old" is, for instance, what Wordsworth read into the old constellation of the oak and the broom, which in Aesop teaches us the advantage that pliability holds over massive strength. On the other hand, playfully parabolic erotic verse of the *Heidenröslein* type became a sanctuary for simple, conventional pseudo-Aesopian plots and skeptical epimythia: "Roses must live and love, and winds must blow"—women *always* love too much, and men are volatile. Both generic hybrids, the typological fable and the fable of erotic innuendo, have not been studied as yet and will be presented and discussed in detail.

As for other variants of the genre, the distinction between fables and parables, as more respectively less commonplace, can still be helpful to indicate different *tendencies* in different functional categories. Humorous, satirical, and didactic texts tend to continue and imitate folkloristic motifs with plain and sober morals affixed to them, whereas fables of the "reverie" type favor a more esoteric imagery and a less univocal meaning. Thus a muddy rainpool in one of Lytton's reveries, covered with ice, "cleansed," "calm'd and shelter'd" by it, bides its time for the return of a star in whose form it once reflected "Heaven's distances divine." Images like this have a rather vague symbolic potential that, at a closer inspection, veers between Christianity and philosophical skepticism.[13] The historical and semiotic aspects of this will have to be discussed.

First and foremost, however, I want to reserve the term "parable" for a specific narrative structure that reorients the reader by leading her or him to deeper insight through a reconsideration of stereotypes. This concept has been introduced by Theo Elm in his recent book *Die moderne Parabel,* which, however, does not treat any nineteenth-century English texts.[14] I have found this normative model, which Elm claims needs transcending in the analysis of *Modernist* parables, an intriguing construct. For it raises the question whether one should not consider theoretical and empirical reasons for departing from it even in discussing nineteenth-century material. For one thing any semiotic model of the fable's levels of meaning, and thus insight, must take account of oscillating signifiers that may work toward deconstruction as a close reading of one of Lytton's fables will show. Secondly one aspect of the fable's development in the later nineteenth century is precisely that it begins to undermine, more or less explicitly, its parabolic, that is, reader-reorienting impact. True the "typological" fable mentioned earlier may be said to rely, to a degree, on this impact—a male lark starting out to seek the "glory of gold" in the sky finds it at home, where the evening sun has transfigured his wife with a glow of "russet gold" (to a degree because even here the signifier "gold" would seem to work subtly against the fable's spiritual signifieds). However Robert Louis Stevenson, for one, when he wrote bitter counterfables in prose, not only subverted such smugness but exploded the whole idea of univocal moral meaning. "Parabolic" texts and their subversions will thus be regarded as specifically structured subclasses of fables.

Reynard's impersonations and our discussion of adequate terms for them have already indicated the direction and procedure of the present study. It will start with an extensive documentation, in word and image, of the abundance of nineteenth-century verse fables and parables in England, with an occasional glance at the United States. Most of the texts are taken from Victorian collections and poetry anthologies in the British Library and the Victoria and Albert Museum, and are presumably unknown. They will be arranged according to function. The fable continued to do service in humor, satire, and education, extending its scope to religious and philosophical speculation—and, much more down to earth, to entertainment and erotic innuendo. There occurs an interesting merger of emblem and verse fable into what (using an older genre term) might be called the "emblematic fable." These texts, at first clearly typological in their Christian reading of worldly things, move in the course of the century toward religious and philosophical skepticism until they turn into a plain denial of life as meaningful. If this metaphysical bent costs them the univocal authority of the older texts, they certainly gain in complexity and emotional intensity. There will be a separate chapter on prose fables, which generally lacked the linguistic subtlety and intellectual sophistication of fable poetry until they, too, in the hands of one of the masters of Late Victorian prose, became, in his words, "something too ambitious, in spite of its miniature dimensions, to be resumed in any succinct formula without the loss of all that is deepest and most suggestive."

Taking stock is only part of my project, however. The outline of the intellectual history of the times, as reflected in fable poetry and prose, be it satirical, pedagogical, or philosophical, will be filled in with richer details in the second part of my study, which focuses on three Victorian books. Here my approach will be semiotic (including theories of discourse) rather than functional or historical.

A review essay of Lord Lytton's *Fables in Song* (1874) by Stevenson contains perceptive remarks on the post-Darwinian fable. Stevenson's paper is at once an apologia of the fable genre and an anatomy of a newly developing variant—away from "old stories of wise animals or foolish men" and toward what the author describes as "emblematic" and "metaphysical." Such tales, "less and less fabulous" in their machinery, take account of the fact that "man cannot deal playfully with truths that are a matter of bitter concern to him in his life." In consequence, they evolve into "quite a serious, if quite a miniature division of creative literature." The fable, evidently, has recognized the importance of being earnest. Stevenson's observations, based on a small corpus, corroborate, from a contemporary's point of view, the main generalizations attempted in the book's documentary section. Their main importance, however, is that they hold up to view Lord Lytton's collection of poems as a work whose narrative virtuosity, humor, and allusiveness rival in verse what Victorian novelists achieved in prose. I will attempt to suggest some of the narrative and verbal charm of Lytton's forgotten volumes. At the same time, my main topic is their ideological project in manipulating the implied (and thus, presumably, many an actual) reader by a skillful ordering and evaluation of discourses. Finally I will make an attempt to analyze one rather complex text within a semiotic model marking off original from traditional fable writing in an attempt to argue that original fables, even if they seem to fit into interpretive straitjackets like that of "parabolic meaning," should rather be observed in the Houdinian tricks whereby they attempt to escape them.

Second in line will come an attractive picture book of the Victorian age, which was created by the artist and designer Walter Crane—an *Aesop* in limericks (1887) with highly sophisticated color plates in what was then the most advanced technique of book illustration. Again on the basis of semiotics, I will this time discuss Walter Crane's art as no less Houdinian. His plates seem designed to escape, by subtle subversion, from one form of illustration—"picturing"—into another—"depicting" or (in the artist's own words) "pictorially pointing." Thus in the context of a rhetoric of *visual* components, the distinction between fable and parable will be seen to break down once more. Although Aesop's fables are certainly "pictured" faithfully, Crane's "depicting" can be seen as creating, so to speak, para-parabolic topical meaning by "pictorially pointing to" variously readable visual material.

But there are more elementary discursive conflicts than those between unruly texts and models which would restrict their meanings. One of them will bring this book to its close. This conflict evolves from, and shows the inherent problems in, the fable's convention of talking animals. Presenting horses, for instance, as capable of speaking like humans does not imply that they share man's multiplicity of discourses—let alone the *duplicity* made possible by the functioning of signifiers like "good," "gentle," "work," or "vice" in (to use a term proposed by Richard Rorty) different human "final vocabularies."

It is true that the spate of Victorian romances written for small children hardly ever showed any marks of tension under their rough-hewn semantics and pragmatics. With the excuse of giving merely an elementary grounding in speech that was "right" and "nice," their language had no truck with ambiguities and internal contradictions, the dependence of all linguistic signs on their interpretants, and the necessity of interpreting these interpretants in their turn. One of them, however, Anna Sewell's classic *Black Beauty,* is based on the assumption that man and beast are divided rather than united by their ability to speak.

Apparently an extended parable about the hardships of life and man's final deliverance from them, *Black Beauty: The Auto-*

biography of a Horse (1877) was harnessed to serve in Victorian middle-class child-rearing, where great emphasis was put on willing submission and self-denial. This was only made possible, however, by its being written around a silent center: the absence of resistance, let alone revolt—quite "natural," of course, where horses are concerned—in the face even of insufferable cruelty: "There is nothing that we can do, but just bear it, bear it on and on to the end." But there are speaking silences, and the book's shifting parabolic outline, as well as its collage of contradictory parabolic insets, explodes much of its seemingly unified meaning. If much of the horses' discourse, though it never really existed, could be overheard in every nursery ("Do your work with a good will"), it is just as true that Anna Sewell's mimicry has written into it much that makes the reader think twice. So *Black Beauty* may, after all, belong with adults' classics like Book Four of *Gulliver's Travels,* which implant into what might be read as fable something of the indeterminacy of the texts we call *Life.*[15]

Fables
Less and Less
Fabulous

Part I
An Abundance of Fables

1

Humor, Satire, Education

CONTINUITIES

THE interest accorded to the fable in the eighteenth century persisted in the nineteenth. For one thing throughout the century the old and renowned fable collections continued to be an important item in the book market. John Gay's *Fables* of 1727 and 1738 remained best-sellers and went through numerous reprints and reeditions: booksellers' catalogs record at least sixty new editions up to 1880. The same applies to the foreign classics of the fable in English translation—for example, the fables of La Fontaine (1668–94) or the more sentimental ones of Claris de Florian (1792), which came out in England in 1806, 1837, 1851, 1861, 1888, 1896, and 1897.[1] In addition new discoveries from former centuries and foreign countries joined the canon: *The Poems and Fables of Robert Henryson, Now First Collected* appeared in Edinburgh in 1865, and Krylov's fables were translated from the Russian in 1869.

These editions, of original or translated texts in prose and verse, were frequently illustrated. The announcement of new or more numerous illustrations made for increased attractiveness, and occasionally the plates were the real reason for a new publication. Thomas Bewick, for instance, who had developed the art of wood engraving to a perfection hitherto unknown, continued to work on his *Select Fables* of 1784 through many editions, and later, in 1818 and again in 1823, he furnished his *Fables of Aesop* with completely new sets of illustrations. Emerson Charnley, the publisher, reacted by republishing, in 1820, the old versions. Later in 1871, 1878, and 1886, the publisher Edwin Pearson again "faithfully reprinted" the original edition.

In 1833 "Job Chrithannah" (i.e., Jonathan Birch) engaged Robert Cruikshank, George Cruikshank's elder brother, for his *Fifty-One Original Fables, with Morals and Ethical Index*. To

James Northcote, "The Lobsters" *Reproduced by permission of Schloß Corvey, Höxter*

one W. Le Gros, the frescoes of Pompeii and Herculaneum suggested *Fables and Tales,* which R. Bentley brought out in 1835 as an attractive volume with twenty engraved plates by F. Bromley. Though Bidpai, "the Indian Aesop," handed down through Arabic and Persian versions, remained a subject of interest mainly to scholars, an early illustrated edition in English, with woodcuts by A. R. Branston, came out as early as 1818. D. Nutt, in 1888, reprinted the earliest English Bidpai version in Sir Thomas North's translation of 1570 with its Renaissance woodcuts as a *de luxe* edition.[2]

"A chief inducement in making this collection," wrote James Northcote, R. A., then eighty-two, in the preface to his beautifully illustrated *One Hundred Fables, Original and Selected* (1828), "was the amusement and employment it afforded me in the way of my profession as a Painter, in sketching designs for each Fable." William Harvey, one of Bewick's disciples, "drew on wood and prepared for the Engravers" what Northcote had designed, and he added vignettes of his own to accompany Northcote's illustrations. This book, much admired for its design, soon went through several editions. But tastes differ and

'Alfred Crowquill', "The Lobsters" *Reproduced by permission of the British Library*

fashions change, and in Julia Corner's edition "in easy language, suited to the juvenile mind" (1854), two artists who worked under the pseudonym Alfred Crowquill were engaged to "improve" Northcote's elegant Georgian drawings in oval frames by inserting them into richly embellished, though rather vapid, vignettes that have an unmistakable Victorian tinge.[3] In the same year, the publishing house of Grant and Griffith commissioned Alfred Crowquill to produce "lithographed hand-coloured illustrations" for a volume of *Picture Fables*.

The interest in illustrated fable editions persisted throughout the second half of the century. John Murray's *Aesop's Fables*, with illustrations by John Tenniel (1848), was reprinted in 1852 and 1858. In 1854 Harvey returned to fable illustration and brought out his version of the fables of Gay, adding a number of vignettes with motifs from Aesop. An anonymous London publication, *Familiar Fables in Prose and Verse by the Most Eminent Fabulists of all Ages and Countries,* with illustrations after Grandville, appeared in 1866. Fables illustrated by Ernest Griset (with texts based on Croxall, La Fontaine, and L'Estrange) came out at Cassell's in 1869, and again in 1874 and 1881. And in 1870, to round off what cannot be more than a fragmentary account of a still greater number of illustrated fable editions, *Favourite Fables in Prose and Verse,* illustrated by Harrison Weir, interpreted Aesop's characters as shaggy toy animals.

Apart from the financial interest of publishers in keeping fables in the market, and the devotion of artists to reinterpreting them, throughout the century the fable tradition continued to appeal to amateur versifiers. Their poetic efforts ranged in time from the specimens collected by H. Steers in his *Aesop ... New [sic] Versified* (1803) through *The Fables of Aesop, and Other Fabulists, in Verse* (J. F. Byrne, 1835) and *Fables Translated into English Verse* (James Davies, 1860) down to *The Fables of Florian, Done into English Verse by Sir Philip Perring, Bart.* (1896). The introduction to *Famous Fables in Modern Verse* (1865) indicates what often motivated these rephrasings:

> Many of the old versions of the translations have expressions in them which at the present time are considered unfit for polite society. Even some of the fables written by English poets in the last century contain expressions which no young lady or young gentleman would now like to use.[4]

Evidently these were still the days of Thomas Bowdler, though the latter had long since died (seven years after the publication of his expurgated *Family Shakespeare*) in 1825.

Those who did not feel a vocation for poetry tried their hands at new prose versions of material from Phaedrus, Babrius, and the Indian tradition. The *Fables* illustrated by Tenniel and Griset advertised "a new version" and "text revised and rewritten." Booksellers' catalogs attest to a great number of unillustrated prose compilations as well, and to their popularity, which led to frequent reprints. Here, as in verse, the intention may often have been (in Brooke Boothby's words of 1809) "to present (the text) in a less ungracious form than it has hitherto assumed in English."[5] But as recent research has pointed out, the motives behind these efforts in verse and prose may well have gone beyond a mere concern about insufficient refinement. Annabel Patterson (in her *Fables of Power*, 1991) has discussed their ideological background in the light of the numerous reissues, after 1800, of two much earlier editions, Samuel Croxall's *Fables of Aesop and Others* and Sir Roger L'Estrange's *Fables of Aesop*.

I have personally counted at least fourteen nineteenth-century editions of Samuel Croxall's *Fables of Aesop and Others: Newly Done into English, With an Application to Each Fable* (1722), a success enhanced, from 1818 onward, by Bewick's engravings. Croxall's had been the standard Whig Aesopic collection of the eighteenth century, speaking out, in its applications, against "Tyranny," "Fraud," and "Oppression" and anchoring government in "civil Compacts" that served the promotion of general "Happiness and Well-being" and "the Establishment of Justice and public Peace."[6] The book had been compiled (as Croxall noted) to provide a correction to the principles laid down in Sir Roger L'Estrange's compilation *Fables of Aesop ... With Morals and Reflections* (1692), whose reflections constituted a "Tory-verging-on-Jacobite statement of political principles" in their support of absolute monarchy (Daniel).[7] According to Patterson the controversial coexistence of these reissues throughout the nineteenth century is reflected in the spate of *new* versions and "revised and rewritten" fable books and their applications.

Patterson discusses, for instance, the Rev. G. F. Townsend's frequently reprinted *Fables of Aesop, with New Applications, Morals, etc.* (1866), which came out first with Croxall's translation, then (1867 and later) was "literally translated from the Greek" by Townsend himself. Faced with Croxall's Whig claims that the fables "recommend a Love for Liberty, and an Abhorrence of Tyranny" Townsend (to quote Patterson) made it clear in his applications "that Croxall and what he represented were the unnamed phantoms against which his compilation (though without stating its purpose) was mustered."[8] On the fable of "The Frogs Desiring a King," for example, Townsend comments that the people of England are "remarkable for their loyal attachment to their sovereign. This fable will be ever popular among them. It inculcates lessons of loyalty, and fosters that spirit of obedience so dear to the hearts of Englishmen."[9] Similarly "The Body and Its Members" is updated by Townsend to signify that "the union of all classes is necessary to that maintenance of authority, respect for the public law, and stability of government, on which the safety of property to individuals and the continuance of the national prosperity alike depend." And he adds, with a flourish and a striking metaphor, an "epimythion" or moral in verse:

> The rich the poor, the poor the rich, should aid:
> None can protect themselves by their own shade.

In this context it is instructive to return to James Northcote's magnificent lobsters, mother and child, depicted above. On the sea-shore they find the shell of a boiled member of their species, which the young one admires as "decked out in noble scarlet." Whereupon its mother, evidently Tory in flesh and blood, supplies the relevant information, adding emphatically, "hence learn from the terrible example, to be humble and content, obscure and safe." And the author, in his application, ratifies the old creature's wisdom, "The superior safety of an obscure and humble station is a balance for the honours of high and envied life."[10] It may not be without political significance that after Northcote's death in 1831, in the changed climate of the First Reform Bill, the Henry G. Bone edition of *The Artist's Book of Fables, Illustrated . . . after Designs of the Late James Northcote* (1845) and the Routledge edition of *Fables, Original and Selected, by James Northcote, R. A.* (1857) omitted this fable.

To round off this first sketch of continuities in fable-related creativity—illustrating, versifying, compiling, and writing "applications"—I propose to glance beyond the bookcases. In their several domains, Victorian artists, craftsmen, and industrial designers continued to make use of fable motifs as well, as they had done in the fable-addicted century before. Scenes from Aesop in particular persisted alongside Greek and Roman, and now increasingly Medieval, subjects as recurrent icons in the decorative arts. Industrial mass production disseminated Aesopian imagery throughout the country. Walter Crane, for instance, an artist and illustrator working as a freelance designer, sold motifs from his picture books to manufacturers of wallpapers, tapestry, tiles, and ornamental plasterwork. Architects used these picture books as pattern collections, so that Crane's Aesopian characters (about whom more in a later chapter) could even be seen sporting on stucco friezes.[11] The J. G. Sowerby Glass Works used Crane's motifs in their molded relief decorations on fancy goods (flower troughs, dishes, vases) made of pressed glass and Vitro-Porcelain.[12] Thus the Phrygian slave continued to serve in many places but he was just as ready to inspire individual artists in the highest echelons. The Victoria and Albert Museum holds an unfinished screen—canvas on wood—which was designed and painted, in 1870/71, by Sir Lawrence Alma-Tadema, R. A. ("Alma-Tad—of the Royal Acad"). It depicts the family of his fiancée below the words of the fable of the bundle of sticks, which celebrates family solidarity.[13]

Ubicumque Aesopus. Little wonder that there was an Aesop in song as well. Hardly any traces have been left of what was presumably a broad oral tradition in music hall and marketplace. These texts, too, would seem to have had their political subtexts, if much closer to the traditional Aesopian implications that suggest political awareness (and, occasionally, cynicism) rather than the conservative moralizing of the anthologies. A broadsheet of around 1810 has preserved a ballad version sung in Covent Garden, in which a gander was given the traditional role of the stork or crane:

> He thrust his poor beak down the throat of the fox
> But he left his poor head there behind him.
> Refrain:
> REYNARD, SLY REYNARD, THE FOX.[14]

Thus, the old fables lurked in many places, yielding models for more original imaginative pursuits, entertaining or highly serious. Three different kinds of *light original verse fables,* whose social contexts can be easily reconstructed, will be considered first before we turn to more serious matters.

FABLE MATERIAL IN HUMOROUS VERSE

Since Chantecleer, the rooster, had made fun of the dreams of his wife Pertelote in Chaucer's *Canterbury Tales* (about 1387), the fable had been part of the English tradition of humorous verse. The nineteenth century continued to produce texts that were somewhere between fable and fabliau. As numerous anthologies of poetry—a favorite product under Victoria—indicate, such texts, carrying mild satire against characters and professions, were frequently recited at social events. Accordingly their tone was one of jocoseness rather than pungency, their objects human frailties rather than moral defects: the vanity of women or the quirks of scholars or men of the cloth.

Lawrence Alma-Tadema, "It Was the Hap" *Reproduced by permission of the Victoria & Albert Museum*

Thomas Moore's "The Donkey and His Panniers," for instance, has as its moral the wise insight that the best help for a donkey that has broken down under its load is to take the burden off its back—an insight that, in this case, is picked up pretty late. In Charles Mackay's "The Beauty and the Bee," it is brazen flattery that saves the clever insect from punishment. The venerable Ralph Waldo Emerson was not above joining the game in verses like "The Mountain and the Squirrel," where the squirrel makes its point with little respect, but much persuasion:

> "Talents differ; all is well and wisely put;
> If I cannot carry forests on my back
> Neither can you crack a nut."

The text surrounding one of these humorous poems illustrates the overlapping of related genres as well as the social function such poetry served. In Thomas Love Peacock's novel *Crochet Castle* (1831), the verses of "The Priest and the Mulberry Tree" are *sung* to the harp at a social gathering—"imitated from the fabliau 'Du Provoire qui mengea des Môres,'" as Peacock annotates. A clergyman, standing on the back of his horse, picks delicious fruit until his exclamations of delight make the horse shy and the priest fall to the ground. The moral:

> He remembered too late, on his thorny green bed,
> Much that well may be thought, cannot wisely be said.

In a topical variant of the humorous fable, events of the day were given playful disguises. An example is J. R. Planché's alphabet fable of the battle some letters fight about the correct pronunciation of the title of Monckton Milnes, when, in 1863, Milnes (poet, politician, and friend of Tennyson and Thackeray) was created First Baron Houghton.

Other fables referred back to Robert Burns's humorous presentation, in dialect, of worldly-wise animals, which itself continued an old tradition of the philosophical animal fable, as in "The Twa Dogs":

> . . . when up they gat, an' shook their lugs,
> Rejoic'd they were na men, but dogs.

As is well known, in the second half of the century Lewis Carroll's parodies, in *Alice's Adventures in Wonderland* (1865), transplanted these animal fables into the wonderland of nonsense:

> But the snail replied "Too far, too far!"
> and gave a look askance—
> Said he thanked the whiting kindly, but
> he would not join the dance.

Like Burns, Lord Lytton, in his *Fables in Song,* made ironical use of the rhymed couplet when the zeal of the petit bourgeois suggested to him its complement in the animal world. Witness the transport of joy felt by a mole in the claws of an eagle:

> ". . . tho' life I spend
> In rising, this," replied the Mole,
> "Was the ambition of my soul."

On the other hand, nine years after *Alice,* Lytton may well have been familiar with Carroll's nonsense ("The Lobster . . . trims his belt and his buttons, and turns out his toes . . . he is gay as a lark"), as his version of a thistle's morning toilet shows:

> . . . And made for himself a fine white ruff
> About his neck to wear;
> And pruned and polish'd his prickles tough;
> And put on a holiday air.

Carroll, on his part, may have remembered Lytton's line (in appropriate meter) when he wrote his fable to end all fables, *The Hunting of the Snark* (published two years after the *Fables in Song* in 1876):

> But the Butcher turned nervous, and dressed himself fine,
> With yellow kid gloves and a ruff.[15]

VERSE FABLES OF SATIRE AND CARICATURE

As in the previous centuries, when writers like La Motte, Arnault, or Lessing had excelled in the production of "original" fables, nineteenth-century foibles and follies called for new fables that satirized them—or at least for revamped versions of the old ones. La Fontaine, who had been available in English since 1734, served as a popular pattern for the creation of new fables with tales like that of "Le Jardinier et son Seigneur," in which "un amateur de jardinage / Demi-bourgeois, demi-manant" implores the "seigneur du bourg" to help him against a voracious hare, unaware that the lord's retinue can wreak more havoc in an hour than "tous les lièvres de la province." On the other hand, John Ogilby's *Aesop Paraphras'd* ([2]1665) was at hand to teach the adept how to insinuate new meanings within *old* constellations, *vide* the French ape, that is, Louis XIV, trying to talk the fox of Spain into cutting his cloak short so that he can lengthen his own apparel with the remnant, magnificently visualized in one of the illustrations to Ogilby's *Aesop* by Wenceslaus Hollar.[16]

Several fabulists followed La Fontaine's generalizing satire on social grievances and ineradicable folly. Sir Brooke Boothby, who had figured in the controversy between Burke and Paine, added a satirical fable of his own to his collection of fable translations *Fables and Satires* in 1809. B., "a man at sixty-three," distills one of his bitter experiences into the epimythion

> Such Sunshine friends I can resign,
> And never for the loss repine.

In 1823 Thomas Moore, better known for his lyric poetry, fired satirical broadsides against monarchy and military in his *Fables of the Holy Alliance*:

> For even soldiers sometimes *think*—
> Nay, colonels have been known to reason.

In 1861 the *Fables and Poems by T.* satirized the greed of the London bourgeoisie. In "The Town and Country Mouse," the town mouse, having declined safer investments, sadly gets what he deserves:

> He put it out to interest tall,
> And now, my dears, he's lost it all.

On the other hand, topical events provoked the fabulists' sneers. A popular title formula of the older satirical fables had been "Aesop at." In 1698 Aesop had been first at Tunbridge, then at Bath, had *Return'd from Tunbridge,* been *at Whitehall* and *at Amsterdam,* whereas 1704 saw *Aesop at Portugal, Being a Collection of Fables Apply'd to the Present Posture of Affairs.*[17] This anonymous or pseudonymous convention continued

Wenceslaus Hollar, "The French Ape and the Fox of Spain"

throughout the nineteenth century. Let me mention only a sharp-tongued *Aesop in Downing Street ... Published under the Superintendence of A* [sic] *Society for the Diffusion of Useful Knowledge* (London, 1831).[18] This tract of twenty-three pages contains three fables that aggressively oppose, from a conservative point of view, Lord Grey's proposed bill for the reform of parliamentary representation (the later First Reform Bill, 1832). One of the arguments put forward is that, once the middle classes were given more rights, the workers would have less security than under the benevolent patronage of the nobility and other big land owners:

> But surely all must think the Ass
> At least is of the middle class ...
> (The worm) its skin were still less proof
> Against the stupid Ass's hoof,
> Than't was against the generous steed,
> That feels distressed that Worms should bleed.

Further *Fables of the Day* came out in London in the same year under the pseudonym of Francis Fitz-Aesop. Here Lord Grey is presented as the more prudent of two roosters ("GREY replied, 'Every bird / In the yard will be heard'"), while a rebellious coal-shuttle indulges in truly inflammatory speeches ("'Remember! We Slaves WILL BE FREE! / WHEN ...'—In came JOHN FOOT-MAN with tea"). In the same social, political, and discursive context, Lord Lytton tells a tale of a steamship's machinery, clearly the working class, revolting against "Privilege, Patronage, Compromise" and destroying, together with the lubricating oil, the whole ship. Obviously the land-owning Tories moved closer together, faced as they were with an increasingly threatening world of donkeys, worms, and dismal figures delivering incendiary speeches.

On further investigation the century offers many more contemporary "sons of Aesop." Even in the New World, the Phrygian slave's progeny had settled, though here they spoke with a different tongue. In 1834 in New York, a review of the country and the times was given by an anonymous *Aesop Junior in America: Being a Series of Fables Written Especially for the People of the United States of America.* As was to be expected, Aesop Junior found the new world no place for privilege and patronage. The book, 238 pages strong and containing seventy-seven original fables, advocated democratic commitment. "The Horse Resolved to Be Free," the last of the fables, tells of a "horse of fashion," his tail docked, his mane cut and clipped, his ears shorn away, who "determine(s) to hie away to the prairies." Having joined a drove of *mestangs,* he learns that their liberty, for which he has yearned, is not licentiousness but has its own rules and regulations, which nonetheless secure a true kind of freedom. The reader is not left at a loss as to what all this means:

> There is a land wherein, some lustrums since,
> A simple people rais'd a state and realm
> In which fair LIBERTY might fairly dwell.

A long epimythion contains a plea to think of the commonweal and make the right use of this liberty.

In the United States as in England, Aesop was enlisted to satirize topical events. In a well-known newspaper fable by Bret Harte, for example, the predatory wolf makes short shrift of the lamb, using arguments that shed light on the political scene of those days (as of ours). He accuses the lamb of having used some influence against him at the primaries. The lamb does not seem to be quite as innocent as in Aesop: "A disturbance of sediment ... entirely local" is its defense, a pun that suggests that there was, indeed, some dirt to stir up. In another newspaper fable, written by G. T. Lanigan, romantic irony (a form of metafiction) is used by the crow clinging to the cheese and snubbing the fox: "I have read Aesop and been there before." The epimythion signals to the readers of the *New York World* that obviously "It Pays to Take the Papers." Lanigan's fables came out as a book in the United States in 1878 under the pseudonym of G. Washington Aesop. Together with the fables of Bret Harte, they were printed soon afterward in London in a pirated edition (*Fables by G. Washington Aesop and Bret Harte,* 1882). Authorized London editions appeared in 1885 and 1889.[19]

A speedy reception like this argues for the undiminished popular appeal of the Aesopian masking (or rather, revealing) of the ways of the world. To avoid piracy several collections of satirical fables were printed in London and New York at the same time. This was the case, for instance, with Guy Wetmore Carryl's *Fables for the Frivolous—with Apologies to La Fontaine* (1898), another collection of bantering fables that had first appeared in newspapers. Caryll made use of speech characteristics to satirize his contemporaries. Here is our old acquaintance, the fox:

"I fear appendicitis."
(The fox was one of the élite
Who call it site instead of seet).

The daughter of the proud owner of "Patrician Peacocks," on the other hand,

> . . . used to say, "You'd reely oughter
> See them peacocks on the mall."
> Now this wasn't to her credit,
> And her callers came to dread it.
> For the way the lady said it
> Wasn't recherché at all.

Fable satire, of course, invited visual presentation even more than the traditional fable—and could occasionally even do without words altogether. In 1857 Charles H. Bennett published in London a volume with the title *Fables of Aesop and Others Translated into Human Nature.* It contained twenty-two caricatures without words in which the artist depicted his contemporaries, judges and court ushers, officers and crooks, in the old clichés of the animal fable. As for the illustrated magazines of the second half of the nineteenth century, they were full of satirical caricatures featuring the fable protagonists. John Tenniel (immortal as Lewis Carroll's collaborator in *Alice in Wonderland*) qualified for his job with *Punch* by contributing illustrations to an *Aesop* by Thomas James (1848). In the eighties, Macmillan's *Illustrated Magazine* published sets of parallel caricatures by the well-known illustrator Randolph Caldecott. While on one page he shows Aesop's hares fleeing and causing the frogs, in turn, to flee from them, on the opposite page it is the directors of a company who, under interrogation, pass the buck to other companies. Caldecott collected and published his cartoons, together with texts of the original fables, in 1883 as *Some of Aesop's Fables With Modern Instances;* I will return to this volume in the chapter on prose fables.[20] In the nineties another contributor to *Punch,* the artist J. A. Shepherd, put on a brilliant show in the *Strand Magazine* with satirical reinterpretations of Aesop. The figures show Shepherd's and Bennett's treatment of the same motif.

Macmillan's and the *Strand,* of course, addressed an educated section of the middle classes. Less sophisticated readers could buy Aesop on two-pence broadsheets with about ten pictures each and couplets beneath; a collection of these sheets, *Fables*

C. H. Bennett, from *Fables of Aesop*

and Fancies, came out in 1884 for one shilling. Even in our days it is instructive to keep in mind what a donkey makes of his master's mishaps with a tricycle (though "secondhand" in those days meant simply "replacing what is firsthand, or natural"):

> Our Ned would tell, Sir, if he could
> What's second hand is never good.[21]

J. A. Shepherd, "While he took possession of the pullet"

VERSE FABLES FOR TINY TROTS

Fables had been used for educational purposes since the Middle Ages. This seems even to have been the case in the schools that the fable animals themselves attended. True we know little about their schooling, so the evidence the historian J. A. Froude gives in one of his fables (1870) is particularly valuable. "Your family," Froude's philosophical cat says to the fox (our old acquaintance), "were always clever . . . I have heard about them in the books they use in our schoolroom."[22]

Although the fables in bi- or multilingual editions may not have significantly furthered in Greek or Latin what is nowadays called *communicative competence,* they certainly extended—more or less entertainingly—their young readers' views of the world. Then, around the second half of the seventeenth century, the fable genre seems to have reactivated its earlier satirical potential, and now *adults* were hailed by "Aesop the Wanderer" (a title of 1704), who offered topical texts full of social, political, and satirical commentary on what went on between Tunbridge

Wells and Whitehall, Amsterdam and Portugal. Later again in a
gradual swing back—at least since Samuel Richardson's revision
(primarily for children) of L'Estrange's politically charged *Fables
of Aesop* (1740)—fable writers once more tended to take younger
readers into account and wrote, for instance, *Entertaining Fables for Little Masters and Misses,* 1747. Such fables, now in
the vernacular, which taught simple goodness and homely virtue
and dealt with social amenities and often sentimental personifi-
cations (*Sentimental Fables,* 1771, *Fables Moral and Sentimental,* 1772, *Fables of Flowers,* 1773) may have contributed to what
has long been regarded as the fable's "decay" or even "demise"
around 1800.[23]

As indicated in the introduction, the report of the fable's death
is, as that of Mark Twain's once was, greatly exaggerated—however much decline there may have been (and I will come to that
in a moment). As a matter of fact, the later eighteenth-century
trends that I have outlined persisted. Undeniably, though, the
readers and listeners whom the fable writers addressed became
ever younger.

For one thing educational verse fables for adolescents, "Little
Masters and Misses," continued to be written. Here, as in topical
satire, eighteenth-century attitudes lived on. This was certainly
the case in the "original" fables that the aged artist James
Northcote (whose Aesopian versions were discussed at an earlier
point) wrote for his *One Hundred Fables, Original and Selected*
of 1828. In an enlightened turn of mind he pleaded for mutual
understanding and collaboration where—as, for instance, in the
case of "Paper, Pen, and Ink"—pride and pretense threatened to
provoke hostilities:

> Then let us all unite,
>   Useless without each other;
> One were not worth a mite,
>   Without his friend and brother.

Toward the end of the century, one of the fable books winning
great acclaim was E. Davenport's collection of original fables titled *Story Poems for Young and Old* (1891). One of its contribu-
tors was, again, Lord Lytton, in the year of his death. In his fable
"The Boy and the Ring," a young boy, after having performed a
marvelous feat as an archer, immediately burns his bow and
arrow:

"Why dost thou so,
Seeing thy first shot hath had great success?"
He answer'd, "Lest my second make that less."

The apparent paradox, a stimulus to discuss the fable's pros and cons, is another trace of the tradition of rational discourse that had characterized most of the fables "for young gentlemen" of the preceding century.

At the same time, much educational fable poetry of the nineteenth century continued late eighteenth-century trends toward homeliness and sentimentality. George Macdonald's fable "Sir Lark and King Sun," in Davenport's anthology, shows how, for the later Victorians, edification was suffered to include a good deal of what now appears as mawkishness. A male lark ascends to the sky to acquire from the sun "a glory of gold" for his plumage. Returning home frustrated and in fatigue, he finds that in the meantime the sun has transfigured his wife with a golden glow:

Glorious was she in russet gold
That for wonder and awe Sir Lark grew cold;
He popped his head under her wing, and lay
As still as a stone, till King Sun was away.

But this is only part of the story. Fables now began to invade the nurseries. With the beginning of the nineteenth century even the toddlers in middle-class families were treated to fables and fable pastiches. We find a spate of titles like *Fables for Children* (1804), *Fables for the Nursery* (1824, 1834, 1845), or *Aesop's Fables for Little Readers* (1888). There occur attractive alliterations like *Fables for Five Years Old* (1820), *Little Fables for Little Folks* (1835, 1861, 1869), *Funny Fables for Little Folks* (1866), and *Favourite Fables for Tiny Trots* (1899). And to top the bill of the plain and simple, we are offered *Aesop's Fables in Words of One Syllable* (1869, 1891).[24]

In a later chapter, I will give an extensive survey and interpretation of infant fables in prose. Verse fables for the very young— a lighter genre altogether, which invited playfully subversive mimicry—had profiles of their own, which I will try to outline in the following paragraphs.

True, where "tiny trots" were addressed, you had to offer simple fare, which may be interpreted as a form of decline. But as will be seen, there is much scope for imagination and amusing double meaning in simplicity. Not surprisingly *The Mother's Fa-*

Otto Speckter, "Billy-Goat" *Reproduced by permission of the Staatsbibliothek Berlin*

bles in Verse, a collection of 1812, reflected on "the difficulty of bringing home to the understandings of children, the moral of a fable," and hit upon the idea of slipping in, in each case, "an introduction explaining the occasion on which it was delivered ... pointing out the fault intended to be exposed and corrected." Her fables thus became little more than inserts in little framing verse narratives, like that of a precocious boy who declines to do any more homework before he is admitted to Eton:

> "O! Edward, hide that foolish face,
> And from a fable learn your place."

Many nineteenth-century fables for the young resounded with rather heartrending noises, which occasionally came even from the depth of the sea. In *Fables in Prose and Verse* (1843), for instance, we overhear a well-behaved little flounder:

> Said the young one, "I will,
> Dear mother, be still,
> I know, by your side, I shall come to no ill."

What now matters to birds and fish is mutual love and homeliness. Family warmth is felt even in cold water. As mentioned in the introduction, Wilhelm Hey's cozy fables and optimistic commentaries, spreading the proverbial golden glow of the evening sun over the child's everyday world, were naturalized, with Speckter's idyllic pictures, as an English classic: "But soon his anger had pass'd away, / And he brought her, for supper, a bundle of hay." Edifying and harmonizing babble like this would, indeed, seem to go flat against the skeptical spirit of the Enlightenment fable, where it is not beyond even the king of the animals to sham illness to have less trouble with his prey.

But one should not overlook the potential for deadpan irony and secret amusement that lurked in the childishness of many of the children's fables. It is difficult not to feel that writing them (and reading them out) must have been great fun. Take the excessively courteous ass in Jane and Anne Taylor's *Original Poems for Infant Minds* (1804):

> "Take a seat," cried the cow, gently waving her hand,
> "By no means, dear Madam," said he, "While you stand. . ."
> And waiting politely (as gentlemen must)
> The ass held his tongue, that the cow might speak first.

William J. Linton, a minor poet (though one of the masters of nineteenth-century wood-engraving), devised limerick versions of Aesop's tales for a picture book which, with beautiful designs by his former apprentice Walter Crane, came out in 1887 as *The Baby's Own Aesop*. For Linton and Crane the fun obviously lay in confronting *Baby* with crisp witticisms true to the older fable philosophy. There was no floundering about in sentimentality for them:

> "So awkward, so shambling a gait!"
> Mrs. Crab did her daughter berate,
>   Who rejoined, "It is true
>   I am backward; but you
> Needed lessons in walking quite late."

By 1887 this preference for wit over cant in children's verse had already developed its own tradition, gaining more and more ground against the importance of being earnest. Recent work in German on English children's books has emphasized this tradition. Maria Verch has shown that around the middle of the century, "when didacticism in verse books for children was generally

Walter Crane, "The Two Crabs" from *The Baby's Own Aesop*

receding," a stream of *antimoral verse* developed. "Serious tone and literal meaning in educational verse were pushed back and parody, caricature, and humor won the day."[25] German classics (readily adopted in England), like Heinrich Hoffmann's *Shock-headed Peter* (as *The English Struwwelpeter* available in English as early as 1848) and Wilhelm Busch's *Max and Moritz*, show that the humor involved tended sometimes to be rather black. Rummaging through English fable books in the British Library, one can find plenty of evidence for this tendency in native productions as well.

The meter preferred for the narrative stance in these poems—
a mixture of cautionary fabulation (for the kids) and ironic detachment (for the adults reading to them)—is an anapestic
three-liner. As it happens this old metrical pattern in children's
verse is identical with the last three lines of the limerick, and
it may well be that it is one of the origins of the limerick stanza,
which Edward Lear popularized in 1861 in the third edition of
his *Book of Nonsense* and whose provenance has remained a
moot point.[26] An early instance of the pattern occurs, for instance, in one of Aesop's well-known wolf fables in Jefferys [*sic*]
Taylor's *Aesop in Rhyme* (1823):

> Said the bird, "It's agreed;"
> Said his patient, "Proceed,
> And take the bone hence, I beseech;"
> Which, after a while,
> And with infinite toil,
> The crane at last managed to reach.

Some of the later limericks' trade in nonsensical linguistic
patterns appears already in *Old Friends in a New Dress, or
Familiar Fables in Verse* (1820), with an ant meeting a grasshopper "pining for want":

> Who said, "Is it you?
> My good friend, how d'ye do?"
> And, "How do you do?" said the Ant.

Whereas this obviously did not aspire beyond a plain retelling
in jingles of what had often been told before, nearly five decades
later the anonymous *Fables in Verse, A Book for the Young*
(1868) had moved much closer to the more sophisticated double
perspective of fabulation and black humor. This is how the latter
book presents—again in anapestic triplets—the deplorable fate
of a rat falling prey to an oyster, which, unable to conceal its
annoyance,

> Said, "This is not nice!"—
> Closed the shell in a trice,
> And it crushed the intruder to death.

That Linton's limericks of 1887 were developed within this tradition is evident when we look at the final triplet of "The Cock,

Walter Crane, "The Cock, the Ass, & the Lion" from *The Baby's Own Aesop*

the Ass, & the Lion" in which an ass tries to chase away another intruder but fails sadly:

> Ass judged he was scared,
> By the bray, and so dared
> To pursue; Lion ate him they say.

Even this highly selective survey has shown, I think, that fable poetry, in its well-established functions of humorous entertainment, satire, and moral education, continued to flourish in the nineteenth century. Over and above this, fable material was adopted by several other literary subgenres of partly entertaining, partly edifying character. From the old fable constellations of animals and flowers, the Victorians gleaned material for erotic innuendo as well as for an emblematizing of religious faith and doubt, of Wordsworthian natural piety, and, at the other extreme, dejection and despair in the face of what increasingly appeared as a meaningless universe.

2

Emblematics and *Vers de Société*

FABLE MATERIAL IN EMBLEMATIC POETRY

In humor, satire, and mischievous fancy, the hidden smile one would like to suspect behind much of the traditional fable's moralizing may often have found its release in open laughter. Two other favorite subgenres of verse in the nineteenth century made use of fable lore, but far less in a spirit of mockery. Allegorical verse of two very different variants—highly serious emblematizing and allusive erotic jingles—availed themselves of the fable code, in which human behavior is, as it were, frozen into a small number of simple and representative patterns suited to teaching lessons of life.

The first of these variants of the fable as allegorical poetry was part of a larger tradition of thoughtful search for divine cyphers in the material world, a "typological" inquiry as Wordsworth described it in one of his flower poems:

> I sit, and play with similes,
> Loose types of things through all degrees.[1]

Where it picked up fable motifs, this allegorizing carried on an old hybrid form of the fable that Hermann Tiemann has named the "emblematic fable." For back in the sixteenth century, emblems (combining a picture, a motto, and a narrative or exegesis of both) had already included well-known fable plots and characters. An example is "Defflance non moins vtile que prudence" in Gilles Corrozet's compilation *Hecatomgraphie* (Paris, Denys Janot 1540)—again featuring our old friend the fox who, out of well-founded suspicion, is keeping away from the cave of the lion shamming illness: "Les imprudens ... sont tout les iours deceus / Comme il appert des bestes cy dessus."[2]

Emblematizing poetry, which is the topic under discussion here, dispenses with the *pictura,* replacing it with a verbal sce-

Deffiance non moins vtile que prudence.

*Le fin Regnard apperceuant les pas
De mainte beste allant à la tasniere
Du fort Lyon,en reculant arriere
Dit à par soy:certes ie n'y vois pas.

Q Vand on veult bien entreprendre vng
affaire
On doit penser à ce que lon doit faire,
Et regarder le dommage ou prouffit
Qui en aduient,comme le Regnard feit:
Lequel passant par deuant la cauerne,
Ou le Lyon habite & se gouuerne,
Cestuy Lyon le conuya de boire
En sa maison,en luy faisant à croire
Qu'il ne deuoit de luy tant s'estranger,
Mais la semonce estoit pour le manger,
Ce que entendoit assez bien le Regnard,
Lequel luy dit,compere dieu me gard
D'aller vers vous,ie suis assez sçauant
Pour esplucher ce qu'on dit bien souuent,
Que qui void mal à son proche aduenir
Comme pour soy luy en doit souuenir.
I'ay veu entrer vne trouppe de bestes
N'a pas long temps au lieu la ou vous estes
Ie voy les pas comme elles sont entrées,
Mais non les pas comme sont retournées,
Dont ie conclus que ie n'y dois aller.
Ainsi nous faict entendre à son parler
Celluy Regnard,que ne deuons ensuyure
Les imprudens, qui par faulte de viure
Bien sagement,sont tous les iours deceus,
Comme il appert des bestes cy dessus.

Gilles Corrozet, "Defflance non moins vtile que prudence" *Reproduced by permission of the Bayerische Staatsbibliothek, Munich*

nic representation. Yet the model of the emblem remains unmistakable. For one thing emblematizing poetry retains the emblem's analogical argument structure, borrowing its correlating formulae of the type "Comme il appert des bestes," or, to quote from a well-known sixteenth-century English collection, "so ofte it happes, when wee our fancies feede" (Geffrey Whitney, *A Choice of Emblemes,* 1585).[3] As in the old emblems ("Lo, Time dothe cut us off," Whitney), the speech act of exhortation is foregrounded throughout by, for instance, emphatic exclamations. Furthermore as in emblems, a second enunciative position may be established through dialogue with the figures or objects held up to contemplation—a metaphorical doubling of the expostulations that adds to their impact. To remind the reader of this model, let me refer to Bunyan's *Book for Boys and Girls: Divine*

Emblems (1686) ("What ails this Fly? . . . Away thou silly fly; Thus doing, thou wilt burn thy wings and dye") or to one of the few emblem books of the nineteenth century, *Divine Emblems* by an author who wrote under the pseudonym Johann Abricht (1838), where the narrator scolds a boy (an emblem of a Christian who has too much confidence in his faith) for mingling with card sharpers:[4]

> Vain, foolish youth!—to think thy mite of sense
> Can cope with such—so consummate in wiles!—. . .
> Thou hast no chance!—thy winning is in flight!

As is to be expected, in emblematizing poetry the fable material undergoes a transformation which situates its ethos between those of emblem and fable. The traditional emblem (according to Albrecht Schöne) depicts the world as static and grounded in transcendence, a "truly universal web of relations and meanings." The epimythion of the traditional fable, concerned with invariants of human behavior, extrapolates from concrete plots and teaches what may be pragmatically favorable and profitable—which, if done with a certain amount of skepticism or even cynicism, may restrict, or even explode, faith in a well-ordered, significant universe. Emblematizing fable poetry, as the result of a merger of the two, while creating, investigating, and contemplating specific plots, nevertheless confirms a meaningful view of the world.[5]

The constellation, for example, of a spider and a swallow that destroys its web and steals the prey was known from La Fontaine. His cynical moral was that those who are clever and strong are favored by Jupiter.[6] Now in 1811 Patrick Brontë (father of the novelists) published, in his *Cottage Poems,* a poem with the title "The Spider and Fly." In this poem a meditative voice observes and addresses ("I see you") a spider building its web and a fly that is caught in it. The speaker in the poem analogizes his verbal *pictura* by means of the emblematic formula mentioned before:[7]

> So, thoughtless youths will trifling play,
> With dangers, on their giddy way.

A blast of wind—like the swallow in La Fontaine's fable—tears apart the web:

> Thus worldlings lean on broken props,
> And idly weave their cob-web hopes
> And hang o'er hell, by spiders' ropes.

Intrigue, complication, and antithetical point, the plot segments of the fable, are clearly preserved. But by introducing an "I" as speaker and interlocutor, the author creates additional suspense which is based on mental and moral attitudes like guessing, encouraging, and warning (where the latter includes the emblem motif of "foolishness" as quoted earlier):

> You cunning pest! why forward, dare . . .
> Ah! silly fly! will you advance? . . .

Thus parallel to the events, a second, interior plot is created. The moral resulting from both is no longer, as in traditional fables, a disillusioned reading of the world as it is assumed to be in the fable code. Instead it grows from a deciphering and interpretation of the details within a "universal web of meanings," which spans from Heaven to Hell[8]—as emblems or "similes," that is, of human frailty and malice, of the thoughtlessness, silliness, idleness, and cunning of "worldlings" who lack, or disregard, God's grace. Significantly Brontë regarded his verses, which he had composed for "the lower classes of society . . . the unlearned and poor," as something quite new: "The Author has not seen any work of exactly the same nature."[9] Clearly for him, fable topoi, as part of the plain man's reality code, could be relied on to give verisimilitude to more refined encodings as well.

Lord Lytton, whose collection *Fables in Song* is representative of nineteenth-century fable, and fable-related, poetry in all its aspects, employed these techniques of emblematizing, reflection, and interior dramatization as well. In a poem of twelve lines, for instance, he scolds a fir tree "bless(ing) its favour'd fate" because it has found an inch of earth between "bare rocks":

> Fool! Thy good fortune was not the bestowing
> Of that scant handful of earth's overflowing.
> It was—and is—thy faculty of growing.

Another twelve-line poem describes the quiet flow of a river, majestic and undisturbed, till a tiny rock pierces its surface, "whereat it foam'd with wrath." As in emblematic poetry, the emphatic formula "Lo!" identifies the simile as a type held up to sight and insight:

Over the depth, indifferent, smooth of pace,
The current with continuous calm had crossed.
Yet lo, a little pinscratch in the face,
All its repose was lost!

The headings of these two *Fables in Song,* "A Provision for Life" and "Composure," plainly give away their character as emblematic fables, whereas Patrick Brontë in his emblematizing still adhered to the fable convention of naming the protagonists.[10]

Encoding the Pleasures and Sorrows of Love

However, the emblematizing of fable motifs was not restricted to ponderous meditation. In a more lighthearted vein, the narrative structure of the fable and a number of its traditional motifs were used as playful allegories of stereotypical erotic situations. In verse of the *Heidenröslein* type, a small repertoire of animals and plants and their relationships were encoded as erotic cyphers. Goethe's poem itself, in its setting by Schubert, may have served as a powerful model, because in the course of the century it was given several further musical settings by English composers, which enjoyed considerable popularity in Victorian drawing rooms. A French poem of this genre that has survived to our days is Victor Hugo's "Le papillon et la fleur," for which Gabriel Fauré did what Schubert had done for Goethe. Almost all the rest of the spate of album verses—apart from some everevergreens like "The Last Rose of Summer," "Time's Garden," "Cherry Ripe," and "The Lost Chord"—are now forgotten.[11]

In those days, however, when recitation and piano playing were the main forms of entertainment at social gatherings, these short allusive poems, often conceived as texts for songs, were published in great numbers. In this context the words "in song" in the title of Lytton's collection may have added to its attractiveness. And those who bought Lytton's fables would hardly have felt disappointed. Not only were a considerable number of the texts suitable for effective recital ("An ass his feelings has, / And the feelings of this ass, alas! / Were wounded"), but they chimed with two powerful conventions of the drawing room: 1) that of evading embarrassing subjects by playful innuendo, because 2) matters of love and sex could be illustrated, as it were in passing, through a set of idyllic nature miniatures.

Thus several of the *Fables in Song* invite the reader to look at leaves of grass in morning dew, sheltering boughs, and insects on flowerbeds, placing him or her in an almost voyeuristic position:

> The green grass-blades acquiver
> With joy at the dawn of day . . .
> And the branches, bending down to the ground,
> A canopied cradle wove him . . .
> All in a flutter of flatter'd delight,
> And vain of his chance, but not trusting it quite,
> The Butterfly dandled his dainty flight.[12]

In this framework of daintiness, one of Lytton's emblematic fables ("Prematurity") coyly develops erotic innuendo into an admonition against premature sexual experience. Look at the young flowers nipped in their buds:

> Which, in haste to be cherish'd,
> With loosen'd zone
> Had too soon to the sun all their beauty shown.
> Lightly-vested,
> Amorous-breasted,
> Blossom of almond, blossom of peach:
> Impatient children, with hearts unsteady,
> So young, and yet more precocious each
> Than the leaves of the Summer, and blushing already!

"Lightly-vested, / Amourous-breasted," Lytton's delicate maiden flowers remind one of Walter Crane's flower allegories in *Flora's Feast* (1889).[13]

Because this undercurrent of Victorian poetry—the fable in dainty guise as vers de société[14]—seems to be little known, a few more paragraphs will be devoted to it before Victorian seriousness finally claims its rights again.

It is mainly the botanical subset of the fable's agents (one thinks of oak and reeds, fir and bramble, thistle and ear of wheat, lily and rose) that were looked after with tender care in the Victorian drawing rooms. Philip Bourke Marston's "The Rose and the Wind" is representative of this kind of fable pastiche:

The Rose.— Already my flush'd heart grows faint with bliss;
    Love, I have longed for thee through all the night.
The Wind.—And I to kiss thy petals warm and bright . . .
The Rose.— O Love, O Wind, a space wilt thou not spare?

Walter Crane, "The Little Lilies of the Vale" from *Flora's Feast*

The Wind.— Not while thy petals are so soft and fair . . .
The Beech.—Broken she lies and pale, who loved thee so?
The Wind.— Roses must live and love, and winds must blow.

It is easy to recognize distinctive features of the fable: meaning on (at least) two levels, nonhuman agents, and a contrastive plot structure leading to an antithetical epimythion. Even the fable's skeptical outlook has been preserved.[15] At the same time, the word "must" in the last line, which, as it were, justifies the ways of Eros to Woman, has an emblematic ring and is quite unlike fable discourse. Compare also Joseph Skipsey's "The Bee and the Rose":

> "You won't!" the Rose's accents ring;
> > "I will!" the Golden Bee's are ringing;
> And tho' the winds, to aid her, spring,
> > Soon with the breeze-tost bloom he's swinging.
> His prize secured, away he goes,
> > At which anon, in rage the rarest;
> "Come back, thou villain!" cries the Rose;
> > "Come once more kiss me, if thou darest!"

which, again implying that "roses must live and love," is a no less emblematic, though much more insidious, justification, this time of Man's ways with Woman to himself.

In a variant of the dominating narrative techniques, one of the agents presents the poem as his monologue. Whereas in Aesop the oak and the reed (or tendril or shrub), exposed to rough winds, had for centuries taught the pragmatic rule that frailty, combined with flexibility, had a fair chance against mere strength, in Skipsey's version a daffodil and a daisy, engaged in a beauty contest, undergo much the same experience:

> Adorned in many a gem this morn,
> A daffodil without a peer,
> I reared my head, and treat with scorn
> A one-pearl-gifted daisy near.
>
> That very hour, lo! wind-a-rock'd,
> Was I left gemless evermore;
> Nay, made to envy what I'd mock'd,
> That one sweet pearl the daisy wore.

Again, with the plot outline preserved, what the poem tests and vindicates is not (as in fables) what experience shows to hold true, but what (typologically) must be true: the pearl clearly emblematizes purity, the daisy meekness, as Christian virtues.

Occasionally the interpretation of a set of nature miniatures as part of "a universal web of relations and meanings" moved beyond love as well as loveliness. The transience of everything beautiful lent itself to fable pastiche in Austin Dobson's "A Fancy from Fontenelle," which used the old topos of the proud rose. She mocks the old gardener, but he, the speaker of the poem, survives her flowering time and finally sweeps aside the blossoms. Obviously "roses must die"—as the epimythion reveals, the core of this little tale is, again, emblematic, here of the relentlessness of Time:

> And I wove the thing to a random rhyme,
> For the Rose is Beauty, the Gardener Time.

To sum up—the "emblematic fable" (as described by Tiemann) lived on in emblematizing poetry whose canvas was the Christian universe, with humanity idly weaving its cobweb hopes and dangling o'er hell (of which, shortly, there will be more from a historical perspective). Meanwhile the "random rhymes" of the Victorian drawing room (like its humorous verses) turned the fable, as it were, into genre painting. By emblematizing fable matter in a different way, smugness toyed with the sensuous and the risqué. What prevailed was not contemplation but nonchalance: this was, after all, how things had to be. The language turned daintily ornate with flutters and flatterings, dandlings and delights. Abounding in sheets of music and anthologies, an early mass phenomenon, these rhymes were genre paintings all right, but paintings in glossy reproduction, charming little transfers.

3

Verse Fables between Piety and Skepticism

RETURNING from a wealth of sensuous detail to the serious business of making sense of the world, the present study will now
move from a chiefly antiquarian to an historical perspective. In
this chapter as well as in the following one, I will try to outline,
by means of largely unknown material, an evolution of the
nineteenth-century fable in verse and prose—a development
that made it "quite a serious, if quite a miniature division of
creative literature." The words are Robert Louis Stevenson's, in
an essay that will be discussed in depth later.[1]

Here "seriousness" and "creativity" need specification. Stevenson's own fables suggest that for him these concepts can be para-
phrased, at least partially, by "religious and metaphysical
unrest."[2] Emblematic verse fables as defined earlier impart insights—in contrast to the traditional fable's pragmatism—into
"a universe of relations and meanings." More specifically, in typological writing, fable motifs become "similes . . . loose types of
things through all degrees,"[3] pointing to theistic or Christian
truths. Now a scrutiny of the material shows that in the course
of the century emblematic fable poetry increasingly admitted
skepticism and doubt. Certainties were being first reinterpreted
and then rejected.

Not yet in Wordsworth, to be sure, "who found in stones the
sermons he had already hidden there," as Oscar Wilde once re-
marked. Wilde's witticism does not, by the way, apply to Wordsworth's stones exclusively but can be extended to include a rich
gathering from a Wordsworthian nature already miniaturized to
wings of butterflies and lovely blossoms. In this way the later
poet laureate certainly helped to produce the staples of *society
verse*. In an emblematic dialogue poem titled "The Oak and the
Broom," for instance, decked out with a "butterfly, all green and

gold" and "blossoms (which are) wings lovely as his own," Wordsworth makes use of the Aesopian constellation, mentioned
above, of bulky tree and frail shrub, for a reflection on the contingency of life:

> Frail is the bond by which we hold
> Our being, whether young or old . . .
> The little careless Broom was left
> To live for many a day.[4]

Generally speaking, typological verse by the greater Romantic
poets, even in the simple guise of the fable, tends to be far less
easily accessible than these lines. Multiple coding may invest
metaphors of light, for example, with much more than their
Christian implications. Take the glowworm in William Blake's
"A Dream," which, as "the light of the world," helps an ant that
has lost its way: "I am set to light the ground . . . / Little wanderer,
hie thee home." Even less transparent, Percy Bysshe Shelley's
emblematic fable "The Sensitive Plant" suggests that the apparent deaths of a gentle Lady (but who is she?) and a sensitive
plant that she has tended (man?) may have been no more than
a delusion of our senses "which endure / No light, being themselves obscure."

But this type of poetry could also be subjected unequivocally
to Christian allegorizing, and in this form it was widespread in
the nineteenth century. In Charles Harpur's "The Cloud," a
poem several pages long that, toward the end of the century, was
counted among the lasting works of the "Sacred Poets," a cloud
as a typological sign of the Savior sacrifices itself for thirsting
man, and

> . . . the blessing craved
> Rested upon the land the cloud had saved.

Richard Chenevix Trench, who was to become Anglican Arch-
bishop of Dublin, was one of the most popular religious poets
of the century. In his poem "The Falcon's Reward," a falcon is
slain when it hinders its thirsty master from drinking water
that later turns out to have been poisoned:

> Such chalices the world fills up
> For us, and bright and without bale they seem . . .

so that man would be lost

> If Heaven did not in dearest love engage
> To dash the chalice down, and mar the draught.

The falcon's "keen watchfulness of love," as the epimythion explains, is divine grace.

It is fascinating to see that around the middle of the century the subgenre of typological fable poetry offers itself as a fine gauge to estimate the increasing loss of faith in Wordsworthian natural piety, Blakeian and Shelleyan Neoplatonism, and Christian dogma. Thus I will select from a spate of material a number of poems that map out the growing distance between "Heaven" and "this world" by means of a small set of recurring images of lofty heights and earthly things. Still, clouds, birds, stars, smoke, and wind abound in the religious verse fables of the time, so that no more than a small sample of the evidence can be given here.

At a time when for many Christians dogma was fading into either vague mysticism or mere charity, R. C. Trench showed, in "The Monk and the Bird," how a friar interprets the song of a bird as an invitation to a kind of "holy mirth" whose sanctity is reduced to an experience of bliss and love wholly *within* this world, hardly more than an exaltation of the spirit:

> Leaving all listening spirits raised above
> The toil of earth . . .
> And melted all in love.

In another of his fables ("The Sparrow and the Caged Bird"), the same author described a sparrow nursing a captive bird with evangelical devotion:

> I felt my thoughts to heaven ascend,
> Such heaven-taught lore to trace,
> And deemed, perchance, this captive's friend
> The Howard of its race.

Characteristically this emblem no longer points to "*Heaven('s) . . . dearest love*" (as it did in "The Falcon's Reward") but merely to a "*heaven-taught* lore"—in concrete terms the selfless devotion and sacrifice of a man called John Howard, who, shortly before 1800, had fought for prison and hospital reforms.

Elizabeth Barrett Browning, in a simple but intensely evocative twelve-line poem, dramatized the problematics of avian mediation between heaven and earth within an even less definite and orthodox religious frame. In "The Poet and the Bird. A Fable," people reproach a poet for his transcendent subjects ("While we are thinking earthly things / Thou singest of divine"—an allusion to John 3:12) and praise the song of a nightingale instead. The distressed poet falls silent—but so does the bird, explaining that its own song had been "included" in *his* "highest harmony." In this, the "little fair brown nightingale" appears to have heaven-taught insight deeper even than that of the "heavenly poet" himself, so that there is a suggestion that its song, too, may have been a manifestation of transcendence. This makes the bird a very distant and rather inscrutable descendant of the Romantic archetype of inspired birds, Shelley's skylark (1820), that "from Heaven, or near it" panted forth its "flood of rapture divine." At any rate, the silence of poet and bird and their ensuing death become a potent symbol of more than one kind of metaphysical isolation.

There is a stark image of this snapping of metaphysical ties in a poem written toward the end of the century by the Poet Laureate Alfred Austin, a former Catholic who had abandoned his faith. In "The Owl and the Lark" Austin tells of an owl that engages the narrator in a debate "if God / Be God, or but a fable." This seems to mark a rather late stage in typological fable poetry—the notion of fable itself being reduced to empty fabulation. The fable-writing poet, however, presents his persona as anything but silent:

> O souls perplexed by hood and cowl,
> Fain would you find a teacher,
> Consult the lark and not the owl,
> The poet, not the preacher.

Not surprisingly, Austin's consultant is unrelated to either Shelley's messenger of "unbodied joy" or Trench's instrument of "holy mirth," that is, of bliss within this world. This lark's Heaven, at best, provides not *vision,* but apprehension, a better perception and understanding of Earth:

> Since I had been to Heaven with him,
> Earth now was apprehended.

REVERIES

Lord Lytton, to return to his *Fables in Song,* has a subclass of meditative fables that he called *reveries.* They, too, reflect the process of secularization, while their imagery overlaps considerably with the image cluster we have focused on so far. Incidentally our material may thus help to corroborate the hypothesis of what Jürgen Link, following Foucault, has called an interdiscourse, a collective language of images, symbols, metaphors, descriptive systems, and myths characteristic of a period's fictional, and even nonfictional, texts.[5] Anyway our discussion need not leave the axis of heaven (or sky) and earth.

In one of Lytton's meditations, a dejected rainpool is offered solace and promise by a star mirrored in its turbid water:

> "Measure thy being's depth by the sublime
> Celestial and immeasurable height
> Of what is imaged in it . . . Thou, too, hast
> Thy destined hour. I will return to thee."

While this faintly suggests the "vision" of the star of Bethlehem and Christ's second coming, the fable's plot projects what Austin might have regarded as no more than a heightened moral and spiritual "apprehension" of man's existence in this world. When winter comes to the puddle, a crystal-clear sheet of ice with "purifying power" cleanses "all it calm'd and shelter'd." Thus the promised return effects no more than a moral regeneration; transcendental experience crystallizes into mere secular comfort. The image of the star had already left

> The conscious waters comforted, as are
> Spirits which . . . have held commune high
> Once, *if once only,* with the heavens above.

"Commune . . . if once only": the medium, an uplifting, comforting contact with transcendence, appears to be all that is left of the Christian message. Like Trench's and Austin's emblems, Lytton's conception of what is imaged in man's depth is in conformance with a well-known aspect of the spirit of the times: one year before *Fables in Song,* Matthew Arnold's *Literature and Dogma* had been published, an attempt (in Arnold's own words) "to reassure those who feel attachment to Christianity . . . but who recognise the growing discredit befalling miracles and the supernatural . . . (by) insisting on the *natural truth* of Christianity."[6]

However, even this Arnoldian anchoring of Christianity in "natural" truth remains a very flimsy affair in Lytton's parabolic verse. More than once he veers toward a more radical skepticism. In "Sic Itur," a tree that dreams of being a wandering cloud ("wrapt in a mystical mantle grey / To mount and pause o'er the world") falls prey to a murderous axe. Burnt up, no more now than "a ghastly cloud" of smoke, it can only scatter flakes of sullen soot over the earth "like lost illusions on a heart that aches / *When hope departs.*" Here even the indistinct message of "The Rainpool" dissolves into hopelessness. In our pursuit of "Heaven" in nineteenth-century parables from Trench through Barrett Browning and Austin to Lytton, we have arrived at a heaven that is no more than a mere mirage:

> . . . (Hope's sorceries) . . . the hankering wind
> Will scatter in the void, between the blue
> *We take for heaven,* the green that once was earth.
> Death's silent answers to the cries of birth.

This synopsis of a subgenre and one of its central image clusters in the nineteenth century finds an appropriate end with Thomas Hardy. His flat voice no longer accommodates the rhetoric of either Austin's cheerful down-to-earthness or Lytton's skepticism. In Hardy's "The Subalterns," a poem that was first printed in 1900, the sky and the wind, illness and death apologize to the speaker for the pain they have to inflict on him— subject as they are to "laws . . . Which say it must not be." Hardy's phrase "they owned their passiveness" sounds like a bitter parody of Wordsworth's *wise passiveness,* a spirit of confidence and trust in nature. Thus in the small domain of the emblematic fable alone, we can observe how Wordsworthian trust and piety, Christian faith, an experience of vague transcendence, a spirit of charity and, finally, different brands of skepticism and resignation supersede one another.

4

"Thank God There Are No Wolves in England!"—Fables in Prose

OF BEES, BUTTERFLIES, AND BOOKWORMS

PROSE was even more prevalent in fables humorous and satirical or instructive, edifying, and philosophical—and, as the century advanced, in their darker counterparts expressing the loss of religious certainties and an onset of nihilism and despair. As in fable poetry, nineteenth-century prose fables tended to mute the eighteenth-century elements of wit and pragmatism and used Old Aesop with greater seriousness for a variety of good causes—often replacing reason and good sense by mawkishness and partisan commitment.

To many the best of these causes—and one that, far more than in verse fables, demanded earnestness and thus the eschewal of tongue-in-cheek plotting and verbal wit—was the task of forming the minds of the young, which now, as we know, increasingly meant the very young. When Julia Corner, in 1854, rewrote James Northcote's prose fables of 1828 "in easy language, suited to the juvenile mind" and replaced Northcote's elegant drawings by Alfred Crowquill's pretty revisions, her volume (discussed in chapter 1) was a rather late contribution to what by then had become an important new sector of the book market.

In his *Fables Ancient and Modern, Adapted for the Use of Children, from Three to Eight Years of Age* (1805), William Godwin, better known today as the author of *Political Justice,* is an early witness to the way the Romantic concern with the infant mind began to modify the conception of the fable. In his preface he reasons:

> If we would benefit a child we must become in part a child ourselves. We must prattle to him, we must expatiate.

69

In consequence his own prose is seductively simple and chatty:

> In the last fable the wolf appears to advantage, and I cannot say but
> that I should be disposed to be of his mind. A wolf, however, is a
> very terrible animal, and eats lambs and sheep and even little chil-
> dren. Thank God, there are no wolves in England![1]

The philosopher, in dire financial straits, had landed a best-
seller. According to the catalogs, Godwin's book went through
numerous editions up to at least 1840. Gratefully the author put
up a stone carving in front of his premises in Skinner Street
that showed Aesop reading his fables to an audience of children.[2]

The new attempts to make the traditional texts much easier
to grasp meant, of course, a loss of allusiveness and stylistic
refinement. Thus, Julia Corner's revisions played down political
insinuations like the old lobster's plea (in Northcote's version)
for the "superior safety of an obscure and humble station,"
which was replaced by a mere rule for goody-goody behavior:
"The desire of vying with others in outward appearances, is a
ridiculous vanity."[3] And where Northcote had shown a judicious
bee settling an "altercation" between two butterflies with a ver-
dict that is as well balanced in style as in content ("you are
both right in your partial views, and both wrong in your general
conclusion"), Julia Corner felt she had to drop the paradox and
give the plain message: "(You) both are wrong, as each speaks
from his own partial view of the subject."

As in the eighteenth century, a mere retelling and adaptation
of the old material, such as in Godwin's and Corner's collections,
was frequently found unsatisfactory. In the domain of the nursery fable, too, the Phrygian slave soon found a host of assiduous
imitators. A great number of "original" apologues and parables
were now written for very young children. In the second half of
the century, they were most effectively disseminated in edifying
family magazines such as *The Leisure Hour*, which was published under the aegis of the Religious Tract Society. This paper
had regular sections of *Original Fables* that featured short and
simple texts which were obviously meant to be discussed in
the family circle and instill in the children's minds a spirit of
trust and hopefulness. For example, take "A Cheerful View of
Things" (1866):

> "How dismal you look!" said a bucket to his companion, as they were
> going to the well. . . . "I enjoy the thought that, however empty we
> come, we always go away full. Only look at it in that light, and you'll
> be as cheerful as I am."

Books of "original fables" for the young were mostly produced by women writers and men of the cloth. One notices a preference for what might be called fable romances which confined themselves to a small number of protagonists and followed them from edifying episode to episode. Their titles tended to be rather prolix about the books' personae and their message. Elizabeth Sandham, for instance, who in 1806 had translated the fables of Claris der Florian ("for the Purpose of Instilling in the Minds of Early Youth a True Sense of Religion and Virtue"), narrated *The Perambulations of a Bee and a Butterfly, in Which are Delineated those Smaller Traits of Character Which Escape the Observation of Larger Spectators* in 1812. While "Miss Sandham's" morals were certainly faultless, the information she gave was not always so. Thus a bee, mourning for a dead butterfly, spends "one whole day in gathering (!) wax" to stop up the crevice that contains the remains of his friend. It is hardly surprising that in these books for small children anthropomorphism often produced highly comic effects, such as in *Instructive Fables for Christian Scholars* (1834):

> "Sister, sister," said another Bee, giving her a shove with her nose (!), "What are you talking about so seriously that you have forgotten to bring in your load of honey?"

As these examples show, bees were still as much the fabulists' favorites as in the days of Isaac Watts ("How doth the little busy bee") and John Gay ("The daily labours of the Bee / Awake my soul to industry"). The opposition of idleness and industry, a staple of eighteenth-century moralizing, was now translated into an imagery more easily accessible to children's minds. Isaac Watts, in 1715, had earnestly warned against the devil's wiles: "In Works of Labour or of Skill / I would be busy too: / For Satan finds some Mischief still / For idle hands to do". William Hogarth, in his prints of *Industry and Idleness Exemplified, in the Conduct of Two Fellow 'Prentices* (1747), had replaced divine retribution by a gruesome brand of poetical justice and presumably scared many an adolescent of his day. Now, in "Velvet and Busy; or, Idleness and Industry" (1834), the scenario, a beehive, looked much more homely:

> There were two bees ... Velvet, though she was so pretty, she was not good; she was lazy ... Busy, who was only a plain brown bee, was at work from morning till night.

Yet this domestic scene, on its surface no more than a mirror of small children competing for their mother's affection, was still imbued with the stern demands for duty and moral improvement that the verses of Isaac Watts had reiterated, as a final allusion to one of his most famous songs reveals:

> My little readers, I hope you will take example from the story you have just read, and
>
> > "Like the little busy bee
> > Improve each shining hour,
> > And gather honey all the day
> > From every opening flower."

Indeed it would be rash to register no more than prattle, prissiness, and a rather drole humor in these fabulations for infant minds. A study of contemporary manuals of parent advice (which will be discussed extensively in the final chapter) has confirmed that there certainly was an increasing tendency, in the early years of Queen Victoria's reign, to use maternal "influence" rather than paternal authority—to teach and oblige by examples of kindness, cheerfulness, and goodwill. But this gentle art of persuasion seems to have had its sinister, manipulative side.[4] In this view it would seem that the beehive offered a particularly suitable set of metaphors. The persistent appeals to be "like the little busy bee" insinuated that the safety of the child's home implied an obligation on its part and that shelter and loving protection were no more than a reward (and a precarious one) for its continual diligence and good behaviour.

This is evident in a six-penny chapbook of fifty-three pages in duodecimo, *Fables and True Stories of Children* (before 1855), specifically in one item that features "The Butterfly, the Spider, and the Bee." Here "the Bee worked day after day" and (correctly this time) "made wax, which serves for candles," while (implicitly in return) "her master took care that she should have a good warm hive, and plenty of food all the winter." More emphatically the Rev. Ingram Cobbin, in his *Moral Fables and Parables* (1832), had arraigned (and seen punished) the proverbial incarnations of idleness, indulgence, and indolence:

> the drones, who had eaten of (others') labours during all the fine season, without ever working themselves, went to the cells as usual, when all the labour was over, and expected to be allowed to have as

much honey as they pleased; but the bees ... fell upon the drones
and killed them, or drove them out of the hive.

Nowadays this is easily recognized as an oedipal scenario, with
honey as a symbol of the excessive craving for maternal love.
Quite consistently the "application" locates it within the most
comprehensive version of "the Law of the Father": "They that
will not work should not eat. God never made us to be idle."
Likewise it seems fitting that, in bee society, the worldly representation of the Lord should never be far away. In one of her
widely read *Parables From Nature* (1855), Margaret Gatty, for
instance, no less outspokenly conservative than Townsend and
Northcote,[5] chooses an explicitly authoritarian plot for two of
her bees ("The Law of Authority and Obedience"):

> "Don't you see that if even *two* people live together, there must be a
> head to lead and hands to follow?" ... Gay was the song of the
> Traveller-bee as he wheeled over the flowers, joyously assenting to
> the truth of what he heard.

Incidentally, Gatty's collection of original fables demonstrates
an almost Carrollian talent for humor and allusion that makes
it stand out from the rest. If once in a while the information
she gives happens to be unreliable, it is at least fanciful: "'You
make me young again,' blushed the worm-eaten Beam (being
wood you know, he must needs blush green)." To represent superior qualities, she clearly prefers bookworms to bees:

> "It is very easy to ridicule your betters," said a strange voice; and
> the Bookworm, who had just then eaten his way through the back
> of Lord Bacon's *Advancement of Learning,* appeared sitting outside,
> listening to the conversation. "I shall be sorry that I have told you
> anything, if you make such a bad use of the little bit of knowledge
> you have acquired."

Variations on the theme of bees and butterflies continued to
be played throughout the century and longer, and even in prose
they occasionally attained the philosophical refinement of the
more delicate allegories that were discussed earlier as society
verse:

> The Rosebud loved the butterflies ... "How wonderful they are!" she
> said to the summer breeze. "They are nothing," said the breeze.
> "Their splendour will soon fade. You can get more good from the
> bees. They are wise and know the secrets of life."

But she detested the bees. They were always talking about their work and their hives.

True to convention this aesthetic rose is plucked in the end by a child but it will be preserved in a bowl of china: "There your fragrance will live for ever." This transfiguration (in Arthur Kelly's "The Rosebud") strikes one as a very late rejoinder by a fin-de-siècle sensibility to the Protestant work ethic that had made the bee its favorite emblem. After all that talking about "work" and the "good warm hive," a discourse of beauty, at last, could claim its right.

HYPERTEXTS

In the last third of the century, another change in looking at life had already left its traces in fable prose. In 1874 Anne Jane Cupples ("Mrs. George Cupples") had published her *Fables Illustrated by Stories From Real Life* in twelve chapbooks with pictures. By now, as the title suggests, *realism* had made a claim even on traditional fable lore. Authors had now done their homework in natural history and preferred psychology to easy moralizing. In Mrs. Cupples's collection, Aesop's tales are supplemented by little anecdotes from the child's environment, which take the place of the familiar "morals": "Instead of drawing the moral, I shall show it in an incident of my school-days." Clearly this increases the demands on the child's understanding and creative imagination. At the same time, the author subtly introduces her little readers to the way fables get converted into stock phrases (as with "the fox and the grapes") and thus to the interdependence of experience and its predetermining patterns: "Poor Grace was reminded by more than one of us, that it was nothing but 'sour grapes' made her say it."[6]

In a comparable set-up for adults, realism was joined by satire. Thus in 1883, Randolph Caldecott, one of the fashionable illustrators of the day (whose magazine work has been mentioned earlier) retold twenty traditional fables and juxtaposed them with caricatures of everyday scenes. Just as the sly fox wins the cheese from a conceited crow, in one of the drawings, Mama, her voice flattered, plays the piano, while behind her back seductive Goldilocks is kissed on the sofa. The jackdaw, recognized by the doves in spite of the whitewash it put on to live in the dovecote, reappears as an elderly reader of the *Daily News,* isolated in his club among devotees to the *St. James Gazette* and the *Morning Post*.[7]

Jane Cupples's and Randolph Caldecott's witty reinterpretations are special instances of the more general intertextual phenomenon of narrative or design as *hypertext*.[8] Here specific fables are meant to be recognized as models of a text that is quite different in its plot and characters. Although they help to constitute its central meaning, there is no semantic repercussion on the model itself, such as in parody or travesty.

Further hypertexts based on Aesop can be found among the spate of story collections that were specifically designed for adolescents in the nineteenth century. Thus the old fables occasionally lurked in the background of short prose romances with their black-and-white character sets and allegorical plottings. Take, for example, Gregson Gow's *New Light Through Old Windows—A Series of Stories Illustrating Fables of Aesop* (1883), a book that updated Aesop in eight short stories of approximately twenty-five pages each. In one story Aesop's starving rooster, who, to his chagrin, finds not food but a gem, returns in the guise of a famished gold digger on the south-east coast of Australia: "With spasmodic strength he bit deep into the gold, and rolling over, lay still."

For adult readers, and within the precincts of domestic realism, parabolic rather than apologic meaning structured the plots of fully fledged narratives when they were collected as "fables." Thus the *Bizarre Fables* by Arthur Wallbridge (1842), a collection of circumstantial accounts of contemporary life with moral conclusions tagged onto them, contain, among other items, a review of life in which skepticism takes over and the Christian truths become doubtful. In this story the parabolic career of a "Wise Fool" is finally frozen into an epimythion which is an emblematic *pictura* in words:

Moral

To gain the best fruits of wisdom, it is necessary to be in the topmost part of the tree. If you sit on a lower branch and use a long pole, your spoils will be scanty and uncertain. If you stand on the ground and shake the trunk, your portion will be only the rotten and the dead-ripe.

It may be argued that in tales like these a merger occurred between short story, fable, and exemplum—slices of life, as it were, so thin that they became transparent for emblematic meaning. As for texts that continued to be recognizably of the Aesopian type, they, too, grew in length and occasionally reached the format of short novels. This is the case, for instance, in J. A. Froude's *The Cat's Pilgrimage* (1870), a fable-novella in four chapters. Conversely Aesopian fables sometimes shrank to meaningless episodes within longer tales; thus, in Victorian fantasy books for children, fable characters occasionally put in a (rather pointless) appearance. This happens, for instance, in Christina Rosetti's *Speaking Likenesses,* where (to quote a recent study of fantasy) a fox "appears out of a La Fontaine fable, only to look at some sour grapes and walk away."[9]

AESOP IN STRANGE GARB

So far we have seen Aesop serving in the familiar spheres of moral improvement and edification. Frequently, however, the Phrygian slave was enlisted in causes at which he would certainly have been amazed. Thus in 1871 the Roman Catholics published, with an episcopal "nihil obstat," a *Christian Aesop: Ancient Fables Teaching Eternal Truths.* (Its author, W. H. Anderdon, had already published a *Catholic Crusoe.*) The rival faction retaliated with *Roman Fables* by one S. W. Brett, which on the title page were polemically presented as *Cunningly Devised to Support the Arrogant Claims and the Unscriptural Dogmas of the Apostate Roman Church* (1898).

Already in 1840 an anonymous "Durham Clergyman" (i.e., John Collinson), in his *Fables, Dedicated to Temperance Societies,* had put Aesop's fables on a par with the Bible: "No book ... with the exception of the Bible has taught more salutary truths." His own aim obviously was to vie with both. Here (to return to our favorite protagonist) is a gallant young bee approaching a blossom:

> He dipped his proboscis into the nectary, and, taking a draught, exclaimed, "O how delicious! how it raises my spirits!" ... till he nearly reached the hive, when he dashed against a bough, and fell to the ground.[10]

Down to the end of the century, the road of virtue was illuminated by *Temperance Rays from Aesop's Lamp* (1900). Understandably Aesop's grasshopper, known as careless and easygoing, was used as a warning example:

Look at the Grasshopper. . . . There is of course honest poverty . . . but the want that springs from drinking, self-indulgent lives is sure to lead to . . . the workhouse—the asylum, where out of 21 000 lunatics, 14 000 at least are insane through drink.

Small wonder that parodists picked up this partisan enthusiasm for Aesop. In George Ade's *Fables in Slang* (1900), a rather battered beauty ("In the Morning she looked like a Street just before they put on the Asphalt") is converted to temperance, and this is the message she leaves with a poverty-stricken family:

"My good woman, does your husband drink? . . . When the Unfortunate Man comes home this Evening you tell him that a Kind and Beautiful Lady called and asked him please to stop Drinking, except a Glass of Claret at Dinner, and to be sure and read Eight or Ten Pages from the Encyclopaedia Britannica each Night."

As regards political satire prose fables had served various causes from the beginning of the century onward. In 1809 Richard Gurney published his *Fables on Men and Manners.* In his preface he resolved to follow an Aesop different from that of schoolroom and nursery. "I by no means agree with those," he wrote, "who imagined Aesop designed his works for the instruction of youth . . . they were evidently composed with a view of the improvement of *men,* and were also intended as satires on the reigning vices of mankind." Thus Gurney decided to dispense with what he called "unnatural fiction," "philosophizing beasts, scientific birds, very sensible little fishes."[11] Instead he told stories like "The Demagogue and the Clergyman." Those were the days of the Napoleonic wars, shortly after Pitt's political prosecution of radicals and his Seditious Meetings and Combination Acts. Gurney, one more in the ranks of conservative fabulists, paints his demagogue as "desirous of bringing about a revolution in the country . . . expatiat(ing) largely on the blessings of universal equality"; he then has his clergyman point out an excess of pride and ambition behind his opponent's show of plainness and modesty.

With regard to English politics Martha Vicinus has shown that the propagandist narratives in the magazines of the Chartists, with their recurring constellations of social injustice, political impotence, and misery, were modeled on the patterns of "fables and illustrative anecdotes" in sermons and political speeches.[12] Vicinus even regards them as "moral fables" in their own right: "The characters act out their parts (Honest Age, Corrupt Parson,

Faithful Child) to formula." Prominent among the Chartist writers was William J. Linton, whom we have already mentioned as one of the masters of nineteenth-century wood engraving and about whose talent in writing limericks much more will be said in the next chapter. He sank his savings in magazines which he wrote, illustrated, and printed on his own. In one of these, *The National,* Linton published, in 1839, a series of *Records of the World's Justice,* ostensibly told by a hardwareman. Here the epimythion regularly turns into a profession of political faith:

> I am a rough plain man ... yet I do wish for a somewhat better distribution of property ... so as to prevent all kinds of pauperism.

Half a century later, in another period of political unrest, William Morris wrote utopian social fables in fairy-tale settings, e.g., *A King's Lesson* (1888). Morris's Socialist League fought for its aims with original fables by Walter Crane. Crane's "The Donkey and the Common" (1895) has, as an epimythion, a key to its meanings that shows how helpful the fable could still be in simplifying and getting across complex arguments:

> Comment or moral is, perhaps, superfluous; but if one should read "natural man" or "worker" for donkey, "land monopoly" for the first master, "capitalism" for the second, we can easily find details to fit "commercial competition," "the industrial system," and "the relation of labour to the employer," etc., in this homely fable.

"This homely fable," in its lucidness, has become a political placard in words, a counterpart to Crane's *Cartoons for the Cause* which were printed in Morris's *Commonweal* (1885–89) and other socialist papers.

Day-to-day politics had always set great store by satirical fables, though generally of a less elaborate parabolic construction. Aesopian apologues, revamped for each particular occasion, continued to claim the readers' assent to what was old and proven. In the election period of 1881, a broadsheet with the title *Aesop's Fables—Cabinet Edition: The Budget—How to Make Two Ends Meet* was issued. The sarcastic *Fables for the Voters,* published at Colchester in 1892, hit hard: "The Mouse joined the Liberal League and soon afterwards died of starvation." Up to the end of the century (and longer), to many Aesop continued to be a purveyor of plain and simple truths, whether homely, satiric, or political.

Walter Crane, "The Vampire"

An Election Broadsheet of 1881

"THESE THINGS ARE A PARABLE"—A GLANCE AT THE CONTEMPORARY NOVEL

To discuss links between novels and fables (Aesopian, or, in the wider sense that we have given the term, including what are often set apart as "parables")[13] is to engage with problems of interpretation. Even if, as in some cases, a discussion can rely on manifest evidence, it will still have to lean heavily on the reader's rewriting of the text. A number of studies have tried to locate vestiges of the fable (or "apologue," as some critics prefer to term it) or claimed parabolic meaning in individual Victorian novels. Instead of summarizing interpretations of a random selection of nineteenth-century texts,[14] I shall restrict myself, at this point in my survey, to two critical essays on the fiction of George Eliot, which show the extreme dependence—even in the face of explicit intertextual links—of apologic or parabolic readings on interpretative hypotheses. I will then propose as a more modest aim the attempt to identify parabolic *insets,* such as, for example, in a novel by George Bernard Shaw—a procedure that, in the final chapter, I will integrate into an overall reading of Anna Sewell's Victorian classic *Black Beauty* (1877).

For P. A. Dale, George Eliot may have felt a psychological need for the security of apologic structures after the ambivalent ending of *The Mill on the Floss* (1860). In that novel, Maggie Tulliver reads Aesop's *Fables* (alongside *The Pilgrim's Progress*) to find guidance in life's complexities, and fails—"the mysterious complexity of our life is not to be embraced by maxims" (Eliot). In this context, it is significant, according to Dale, that Eliot's story "Brother Jacob" (written later in the same year) is undoubtedly an experiment in fable writing "in the specialized sense of the word, familiar to us in Aesop's practice." The author invents her hero Faux (the "Fox") as a type who, in his egoism, represents utilitarianism and laissez-faire economics—treating in this "apologic fiction" much the same question that underlies *The Mill on the Floss*—the undermining of an organic society, a community of love. Eliot was able to reevaluate the fable because she had "perceived an essential connection between La Fontaine's purpose" of showing how little human behavior depends upon reason (being motivated ultimately by subrational impulses like that of animals) and the science of her own day, when physiological psychology (G. H. Lewes, Herbert Spencer) was undercutting a scientific philosophy of morals. Somewhat surprisingly, Dale claims that "the act of writing in the apologic form . . . carries for George Eliot an intrinsic value of its own, which enables, leads towards, the possibility of the optimistic, love-directed interpretation of life she is attempting to validate." Thus after "this not, after all, so 'trifling' experiment in the mode of La Fontaine," she can ultimately evince, as in Romola, "a new faith in symbolic expression."[15]

With regard to a parabolic reading, Barbara McGovern has suggested that, in *Middlemarch,* George Eliot reflects two levels of her narrative art—that of "the presentation of facts, of objective reality" and that of "the narrator's attempt to understand that reality"—in the suggestive image of a pier-glass which is "multitudinally scratched in all directions."

But place now against it a lighted candle . . . and lo! the scratches will seem to arrange themselves . . . it is only your candle which produces the flattering illusions of concentric arrangements. . . . These things are a parable.

Or rather, to correct the Victorian author, they are a simile or an emblem, because the plot is no more than rudimentary.[16] Of course this image recurs in Dorothea's realization that Casaubon "had an equivalent centre of self, whence the lights and shadows must always fall with a certain difference," so that McGovern can claim that it is a structuring principle of the novel's plot ("the growing embodiment in Dorothea of [a] process of imaginative sympathy") and of one of its themes (that "each of the lovers [Dorothea and Ladislaw] must . . . struggle to reconcile his perceptions with the other's"). The critic concludes that, finally, a similar development of imaginative sympathy in the narrator turns the novel itself into the parable the author has claimed her simile to be.[17]

With Shaw's didactic fiction, we are, perhaps, on safer ground. In *An Unsocial Socialist* (1884), for example, we find a specific type of parabolic inset that condenses and gives a pointed expression to the novel's theme. Thus in a one-page tale within the tale, one of the characters explains the terms "value in use" and "value in exchange." He tells of the compunction that a painter named Brown feels about profiting from the increment in value that has accrued to one of his paintings after several years. "What a noble thing," the hearer of the tale remarks—which, predictably, is a cue for Shaw to confront the sentimental moralizing of his age with common sense:

> "Heroic—according to nineteenth-century notions of heroism. Voluntarily to throw away a chance of making money! that is the *ne plus ultra* of martyrdom. Brown's wife was extremely angry with him for doing it."[18]

Henry James is an interesting witness to the extent parabolic intent dominated the conception even of *morceau de vie* narratives toward the end of the nineteenth century. It "must be an idea. . . . Can't be a "story" in the vulgar sense of the word. It must be a picture; it must illustrate something," he ruminated on the execution of "The Real Thing" (1893), in which the protagonists learn what amounts to a downright epimythion, "the perverse and cruel law in virtue of which the real thing could be so much less precious than the unreal."[19]

"Too Ambitious to Be Resumed in a Formula"

Admittedly, these are no more than rough cuttings from the tapestry of Victorian apologic and parabolic prose—educational, parodistic, social, political, and imaginative. To conclude this chapter, I intend to give up the synoptic stance and study the art of the fable as it was practiced, in a way very different from what we have seen so far, by one writer who worked during the last decades of the century. The material discussed will indicate the distance he went. I think there is good reason to say that Robert Louis Stevenson set out to question the groundwork on which the fable rests—easy access from the figurative to the literal, the literal meaning as univocal, and "truth" as a set of stable social and moral codes.

Stevenson's short story "Will o' the Mill," written in 1877 and published in 1887 in the collection *The Merry Men and Other Tales and Fables,* is evidently one of the fables mentioned in the title. Intriguingly, it establishes an aporetic form of parody in the fable genre, going beyond mere hypertextuality as discussed earlier, a nonprovocative writing along the plot contours of an earlier text.[20]

It has gone unnoticed that this tale, which has left many readers dissatisfied, is a counterplea (but is it?) to one of Lord Lytton's verse fables, "The Blue Mountains; or, the Far."[21] For Lytton a lifelong yearning for "the far" comes to an end in an experience that may, indeed, be a step toward wisdom (though a rather commonplace one). Seen from far away, from the "blue mountains" of one's dreams, the home one has left behind has become another enchanting item of "the far." In conformity with what has been claimed as the reader-reorienting structure of the *parabolic* fable (Theo Elm),[22] a commonplace (and rationally defensible) preconception is dislodged in the narrative process, while the reader, through an appeal to his judgment, is nudged into accepting a modified position. True "the far" is eternally seductive, and traveling makes a man wiser—but seduction may have blinded one to what lies near, and wisdom may reveal the endlessness of desire.

Lytton's verse fable deploys this familiar way of conducting the reader, although linguistic sophistication makes it stand out from the standard fare of prose fables as described. Stevenson's prose tale, however, goes one better. In a comparable situation, Stevenson's protagonist *denies* himself the experience of Lytton's main character. "In an ecstasy of longing," he is "sick as if for home (!)"—a daring ambiguity that freezes the plot. Indeed nothing much happens. Will is told what amounts to Lytton's fable in a one-sentence version: "Those who go down into the plains are a very short while there before they wish themselves

heartily back again." Against this he specifies (again ambiva-
lently) the seduction he feels "[to] live [his] life." Yet he stays at
the Mill and never moves. When he falls in love and proposes
to the girl, he avoids her rather than seeking her out. Then, to
preserve the quiet of his mind, he breaks off the engagement:
"I have made up my mind it's not worth while." Even when he
resumes his courtship, the alternatives do not much concern
him, "It was nearly the same to him how the matter turned out."
It is just as well for him that the girl declines: "We should be . . .
nothing like so happy." He dies at seventy-two, a contented
man—or so it seems.

The story appears to nod agreement to the conclusion Lord
Lytton gave to his. But then one of Will's later sayings is: "I am
a dead man now, I have lived and died already," and the narrator's tone, deadpan as that in Joyce's *Dubliners* (1914) more
than thirty years later, implies that this is a tale of failure and
paralysis. Admittedly there is nothing so crude as the break-
down and *anagnorisis* of Marcher (another nonmover, despite
his ironic name) in Henry James's comparable plot in *The Beast
in the Jungle* (1903). In this Stevenson would appear to be the
more modern artist of the two. The reader of his "fable," willing
to play the game and see his or her commonplaces either cor-
roborated or modified, is left at a loss as to what "the author
means to say." This may account for the dissatisfaction felt by
the critics that was mentioned earlier. "Will o' the Mill" may have
been consciously designed as one of the fables that (in the words
of Stevenson's anatomy of contemporary fable writing) have "be-
gun to take rank with all other forms of creative literature, as
something too ambiguous . . . to be resumed in any succinct
formula without the loss of all that is deepest and most suggestive in (them)."[23] Seen within Stevenson's oeuvre, Will's Bartle-
bylike abstention from acting points to a first tear in the web of
meanings that ought to define man's place and responsibilities
in the world.

Stevenson wrote several other more traditional (i.e., less real-
istically elaborated) fables. As mentioned before he did not publish them in his lifetime; they appeared posthumously in 1896.
He had started working on them in 1887, shortly after finishing
his famous allegorical tale *Dr. Jekyll and Mr. Hyde,* of which
(according to Edmund Gosse) "they were intended to be, in some
measure, the supplement."[24] Be that as it may—Stevenson's
later fables show even more poignantly than "Will o' the Mill" a
clouding of the traditional parable's transparency.

In "The Sinking Ship," for example, different modes of behavior on board a sinking ship could, at first sight, be easily read as allegories of differing outlooks on the precariousness of life. This is, in fact, the captain's interpretation of his own stoic attitude when he asks his lieutenant to have a shave, "To the philosophic eye there is nothing new in our position: the ship (if she is to go down at all) may be said to have been going down since she was launched." So far the parable seems intact. Commonplace behavior is "made strange," while extravagance has its arguments. Then, in the powder magazine, the officers find an old salt smoking his pipe. The captain reads this as another case of losing *la contenance* ("I should despise the man who . . . should omit to take a pill or to wind up his watch"). But all at once, a sudden reset of perspectives occurs when the lieutenant asks:

> "I beg pardon, sir. . . . But what is precisely the difference between shaving in a sinking ship and smoking in a powder magazine?"
> "Or doing anything at all in any conceivable circumstances?" cried the Captain. "Perfectly conclusive; give me a cigar!"

This is, of course, if conclusive, the opposite of what was intended by his interlocutor. While the officer sarcastically implores both men to look at the situation with more common sense—only a fool would increase the danger of his situation— the captain interprets his "What is the difference?" as "Nothing matters any more."

This amounts to a juggling with proposals to the reader as to how *she* might decide to respond in the predicament: with stoicism, heroism, or defeatism. In the word "conclusive," there is a clash of two discourses that appear equally absurd. The officer's solicitude to reduce risks when, in fact, all is lost, makes him a caricature of duty and strengthens the captain's point, while the captain's philosophy of "nothing matters" refutes itself on the spot through its own incendiary consequence. The ship, of course, explodes, and with it the traditional idea of the parable, which has no truck with undecidability.

In a more lighthearted variant of Stevenson's *Fables,* the moral stance (or, in a different critical discourse, the positioning of the reader) is subverted by one of the devices of Romantic irony, the fiction that the characters know about their own fictionality. In "The Persons of the Tale," Stevenson, who had had a strict Presbyterian upbringing, uses this device to satirize predestination and free will. In a dialogue that two of the characters of his own book, *Treasure Island,* have while the author is supposed to be taking a rest, the subject is Good and Evil (and Divinity: "Were you never taught your catechism? Don't you know there is such a thing as an Author? . . . Don't you believe in a future state?"). Captain Smollett ("the Author respects me") and John Silver, the villain of the tale (but, in his own words, "his favourite chara'ter"), cannot come to terms about their emblematic meanings: "Which is good and which bad?" (Silver)— "(The Author)'s on the right side" (Captain Smollett). The sarcastic point is that, with the ink bottle reopening, Silver's vanity and the captain's self-righteousness will prove equally irrelevant. It remains a moot point whether, in the text called *Life,* what counts is moral categories or simply a good yarn.

As in this case Stevenson again and again aims his sarcasm at church doctrines, which, in his youth, he had repudiated during bitter conflict with his parents. "The yellow paint," in the fable of that name, is daub representing church membership. One of the author's most powerful texts is "The House of Eld." Though furnished with an epimythion, it is anything but (to use Stevenson's own word)[25] "determinate," because the plot and its epimythion ("Beware!") are at odds with each other. *Courage* (to pull out the roots of superstition) clashes with *charity* (taking care of, and treating gently, one's deeply religious parents):

> Beware! the root is wrapped about
> Your mother's heart, your father's bones.

Unlike Will o' the Mill, the protagonist of "The House of Eld" *does* act, and unlike the captain of the sinking ship, he accepts responsibility. The strategies of the text clearly offer intellectual integrity, determination, and persistence in fighting Evil as positions craving the reader's assent. The protagonist believes that what he sees in front of him—the images of his parents—is merely a delusion due to magic. But when he acts to break the spell, he does in fact plunge his sword into their bodies. He loses the gyve which has fettered one of his legs, but the people he meets now wear a different one, declaring it is "the new wear, for the old was found to be a superstition." Again, you can't win.

What appears to be an epimythion is in fact *paramythic,* scintillating in an undecidability that mirrors the hero's double bind. This indeterminacy is structural in that, whichever reading may be preferred, the text exposes it as an *aporia,* a way one cannot walk.

Theo Elm, in the book already mentioned, *Die moderne Parabel,* has suggested that what defines the *modern* parable of our century (Rilke, Kafka, Beckett) is not just that it discredits and holds up for revision seemingly incontrovertible views and interpretations of reality but that it refuses to establish stable meanings, frustrates cognition and understanding, and propagates aporetic thinking, a "liberation of thinking, which no longer fades away into truth."[26] If this analysis is correct, Robert Louis Stevenson has certainly prepared the ground.

Part II
The Semiotics of Fable Discourse: Three Books

5

Lord Lytton's *Fables in Song* (I): The Source of R. L. Stevenson's Theory of the Nineteenth-Century Fable

THE CONCEPT OF THE "POST-DARWINIAN FABLE"

In the last two chapters, this study has moved from a synopsis of texts toward the interpretation of individual fables. At the same time, two fable writers of exceptional rank, Lord Lytton and Stevenson, have been given increasing prominence, while two artists who created one of the most attractive books of Aesopian fables, Walter Crane and William J. Linton, have at least put in a few appearances. The next three chapters are devoted to semiotic analyses of Lytton's *Fables in Song* (1874) and Crane's and Linton's *The Baby's Own Aesop* (1887), before the present scope is slightly enlarged to include a work of novel-length which transposes fable material into the *romance*-genre, Anna Sewell's *Black Beauty* (1877). First, however, Stevenson's views of the contemporary state of the fable in England, which have already been quoted for their perspicacity, will be summarized.

In 1874 Robert Louis Stevenson, at that time a twenty-four-year-old law student completely unknown to the literary world, managed to publish a critical essay on "Lord Lytton's Fables in Song" in the *Fortnightly Review*.[1] Its editor, John Morley, was, at thirty-six, already one of the Victorian Men of Letters, the author of books on Burke, Voltaire, and Rousseau. On friendly terms with Lord Lytton, Morley had first printed his fables separately in the *Fortnightly*. When they appeared in book form, he praised them as "full of fancy, fancy of an original sort, and full of sound meaning ... the verse and form most brilliant ... their spirit and fire ... of the very best, swift, sustained, light-winged, penetrating."[2] Obviously the young Stevenson—uneasy about his law studies while having to face his parents' strong objections to his literary leanings[3]—had grabbed at the chance to see his name in print. His article is mainly a friendly discussion of the merits and occasional shortcomings of individual fables. But although politely chiming with Morley's enthusiasm, his essay goes far beyond the latter's suavity and complaisance and presents a remarkable hypothesis about recent changes in the fable genre which, more than a century later, may help to initiate a rediscovery and new estimation of the nineteenth-century fable.

Where Morley gets carried away into the tritest of mixed metaphors for poetic sublimity ("light-winged, penetrating fire"), Stevenson concentrates on the implications of some of the more sombre of Lytton's fables. He points out a recent tendency of the genre to incorporate, in a "realistic way," "unanswerable problems of life." Where, for instance, it deals with a well-meant action triggering off a chain of catastrophic events, it is likely, according to the young critic, to raise in its readers "white-hot indignation against some one"—which may be read as an impeachment of the "President of the Immortals" about two decades before Hardy's *Tess of the D'Urbervilles* came out. To the *Fortnightly*'s subscribers, these would have seemed rather unfamiliar features of the fable genre, and most readers today would still agree. Stevenson's characterization is part of a more general defense of the fable, in the course of which he gives a rough sketch of its evolution in the course of the nineteenth century. His argument, itself Darwinian, takes account of a spirit of the times deeply affected by the more provocative theses of Darwin, whose *Descent of Man* had been published only three years before.

In 1874 the fable, in Stevenson's view, could no longer be what it had originally been—"of a conception purely fantastic," a bit trivial, somewhat playful, "old stories of wise animals or foolish men . . . the point of the thing (being) a sort of humorous inappropriateness." Rather, as soon as men—in the light of the theory of evolution—had learnt "to suspect some serious analogy underneath," it had "to degenerate in conception from this original type" and lose its pleasantry: "a comical story of an ape touches us quite differently after the proposition of Mr. Darwin's theory." Playfulness and fantasy were bound to fade out while

> . . . with more sophisticated hearers and authors (,) a man is no longer the dupe of his own artifice, and cannot deal playfully with truths that are a matter of bitter concern to him in his life.

Still short and moralizing, valuing intellect over emotion, the fable now, according to the young critic, leaned on *analogies,* not *humorous situations*—"less and less fabulous" in its machinery, it had become "quite a serious, if quite a miniature, division of creative literature." "The term Fable is not very easy to define rigorously," as the essay states (or rather, understates), but it is clear that on the fabliau-fable-parable balance beam Stevenson shifts the weights with a rigorous jerk toward the side of the parable.[4]

Looking back over more than a hundred years, it is fascinating to see the young critic of 1874, at one point, assume a modernist, and arguably even a postmodernist, stance. Quite briefly, rather as an afterthought, Stevenson proposes that the more "serious" the fabulist becomes, the less determinate his moral turns out to be. Engrossed in Walter Pater and well read in contemporary French literature, the 'avant-garde' critic of the seventies claims for a genre conventionally defined by its clarity and rationality an aesthetics of ambiguity, suggestiveness, and, possibly, an in-built *indeterminacy:*

> And step by step with the development of this change, yet another is developed: the moral tends to become more indeterminate and large. It ceases to be possible to append it, in a tag, to the bottom of the piece, as one might write the name below a caricature; and the fable begins to take rank with all other forms of creative literature, as something too ambitious, in spite of its miniature dimensions, to be resumed in any succinct formula without the loss of all that is deepest and most suggestive in it.[5]

In short, Lytton's *Fables in Song* may claim to be Fable Poetry.

Shortly afterward Stevenson himself began to write his prose fables, whose "ambition," "suggestiveness," and "indeterminacy" have already been analyzed. It is easy to see that as a writer of fables Stevenson took for his starting point Lytton's two volumes of *Fables in Song.* I would like to suggest that, for their linguistic versatility and their range of attitudes between amusement and despondency, Lytton's sixty fables deserve being retrieved from oblivion, too.

Because few readers will be familiar with these texts, a few remarks on their form and content, accompanied by examples, seem to be called for. Over and above that, the following account will be structured along two lines of theoretical interest. First I will try to analyze the subtle strategies they deploy to nudge their readers, with the gentle compulsion of what would generally have been regarded as common sense, into a set of shared assumptions, that is, to position them as political subjects. With fables, one of the most blatantly educational of all genres, this approach is certainly appropriate. However it means telling only half the tale. For, as Stevenson notes, with a strategic bow to the texts' "kindly and consolatory spirit"—words that, I think, need some qualification—"throughout all these two volumes . . . there is much practical skepticism, and much irony on abstract questions." This would seem to indicate a semantic space where obvious messages may undergo a subtle subversion. And indeed they do. There is ample evidence of Lytton's veering between a "kindly consolatory" and a deeply ironic attitude, but it is only within a more technical inquiry into the fable's multiple levels of meaning and the "two faces of the order that governs its world" (Needler) that this ambivalence can be pursued into the self-deconstructing processes of individual texts.

Setting the Stage

Of the numerous bearers of the family names Bulwer and Lytton, only one is still known to a broader readership today: Edward George Bulwer-Lytton (1803–73), who wrote the international bestseller *The Last Days of Pompeii* (1834). The name of the author of the *Fables in Song,* however, who was his son, has sunk almost without trace.

Like his father, Edward Robert Bulwer, first earl of Lytton (1831–91), was conspicuous in the political life of his day. After a career in the diplomatic service, he became viceroy of India (1876–80) and later British ambassador to Paris. Again like his father, he craved literary renown. Under the pseudonym of Owen Meredith, he published several volumes of poetry, which echo the voices of Byron, Tennyson, Browning, and Swinburne—among them self-critical lines under the title "Last Words of a Sensitive Second-Rate Poet" (1868). Ironically it was this instance of sensible sensitivity that secured him whatever claim to immortality he may have: Swinburne chose to parody them in his *Heptalogia* under the title "Last Words to a Seventh-Rate Poet."[6]

Lord Lytton's *Fables* begin with a topos of dream visions: the sleeper finds a guide through events that invite an allegorical reading. The narrator, lost in the woods ("Had I miss'd my way? It would seem so"), has fallen into a pit. Like Lewis Carroll's Alice

Marcus Gheeraerts, *De warachtighe Fabulen der Dieren*

nearly a decade earlier ("Down, down, down"), he has arrived in
a subliminal world between waking and dreaming:

> Down with it, down, I fell
> Into the depth of a dell
> Sunless and silent and deep
> As the dim caverns of sleep.[7]

—or (to anticipate) between two sets of verisimilitudes. This is,
of course, a very old professional trick of having your cake called
truth while delighting your readers with feeding them on im-
probabilities. In the dell, caught like the narrator, tarries a fox.
The man invites him to step on his shoulder to escape. Readers
of fables will recognize the variant of an Aesopian constellation.[8]
In this magic world ("a forest enchanted"), man and beast con-
verse freely like Aesop's protagonists or the characters of legends
and myths.

The fox introduces himself as "the ancient Fox of Fable." He turns out, though, to be very much a nineteenth-century character, fuzzy in his metaphysics, demythologizing, while up to his ears in the rhetoric of romantic pantheism:

> "Aesop . . . never having been born,
> He never hath died . . .
> Aesop is living today."
> "Where prithee?" "In me: in thee:
> He lives in each living creature
> (Man, beast, bird, blossom, and tree),
> And his life is the love of nature . . .
> A false Aesop you form'd, of your own,
> We, the children of Aesop, withdrew.
> For we found that to leave you alone
> Was then all you had left to us . . .
> Safe we dwell, out of your view . . .
> They fail not to find us, who seek,
> Though disguised do we go among men . . ."

Rhetoric foregrounds the parabolic impact of the Aesopian scenario. Within the antithesis of "to leave you was all you had left to us," the paronomasia subtly hints at what is implied in the paradox of a form of withdrawal that means remaining present—namely, having been deserted in the first place, in a deeper sense of the word, by modern man in a state of existential and imaginative sterility.

The arguments of the fox may sound rather stagy, but Lytton should never be taken at face value. The disgruntled fox, "ancient" in two meanings of the word, clearly uses (and is possibly meant to present in an ironic light) a still topical discourse which accused modern man of a state of existential and imaginative attrition in images of divine withdrawal. One may think of Blake's "And did those feet in ancient time / Walk upon England's mountains green" or of the Coleridgean paraphrase of Schiller: "The intelligible forms of ancient poets / The fair humanities of old religion . . . /All these have vanished. / They live no longer in the faith of reason."[9] This was, after all, the time when Calvert, Palmer, and Richmond, followers of William Blake, called themselves "The Ancients." The author is setting his stage for an ironic scenario in which reason (and, as will be shown, "realism"), depending on the reader's "faith," may or may not claim an authority ("true Aesop", as it were) that goes beyond mere poetical fancy.

What Lytton achieves in this mode of half-playful, half-serious storytelling is a refashioning of the traditional fable into a much more suggestive verbal artifact. Entertaining, richly allusive, but nonetheless thoughtful, his fables-in-song give new standing to a well-nigh exhausted genre.

PASTICHE AND PUNNING

Verbal wit, a sheer exuberance of linguistic play, is a vital part of this project. The fables abound in allusion and pastiche. Falling rain, for instance, is mimicked in the dactyls of Shelley's "The Cloud", or their echoes in Swinburne:

> Merrily, mockingly laugh'd the light Shower:
> "O fools! lo, I sprinkle a silvery twinkle
> Of beads from my bosom, and where is your power?"

A stag is fittingly sculpted in Keatsian couplets rich in enjambement and sprinkled over with occasional quaintness:

> Nature hath given the Stag a wondrous gift.
> Love, and the force that loving hearts doth lift
> To lofty courage by the sweet desire
> Of winning love, have with creative fire
> Gone to his burning brain, and thence burst out.

And what could be more fitting to depict childhood innocence than the Wordsworthian tone of infantine joy?

> A little child, scarce five years old,
> And blithe as bird on bough;
> A little maiden, bright as gold,
> And pure as new-fall'n snow.

A polished item of table decoration is crystallized in Augustan satirical couplets:

> Bohemian born, but by laborious art
> To perfect polish smooth'd in every part,
> And form'd to shine with frigid grace, acquired
> From that hard lucid style that's most admired,
> A Water-Bottle of the last design
> Glitter'd among the flowers and dishes fine . . .
> Whence comes he? Talk of Form, indeed! O fie,
> The clumsy sloven! what vulgarity!

Moreover Lytton indulges in humorous paronomasia, the playing around with ambiguities of speech and spelling. Every fable
(a borrowing, this, from Lewis Carroll) has to have "a moral tail."
A thistle falls victim to the sweep of a scythe—"One may lose his
head. . . . But I'm on my guard . . . to keep alive." The denizens of
the sea are proud of their president: "Gracing our President's
Chair to see / Such a pearl of an oyster!" Who would not sympa-
thize with the pragmatic philosophy of a carp: "'Stop thy wail,' /
The Carp said, 'Carpe diem!'" A fat lot of good this philosophy
turns out to do for him—Lytton loves the pointed tale (or tail):
"Sage or simple, fish / Come to the frying-pan."

NARRATOR AND NARRATEE

Much verbal play thus sweetens the pills of serious reflection.
In his reveries Lytton presents, in varying meters, meditations
of both living creatures and inanimate objects—that of a tortoise, for example, in an eagle's claws ("A Haughty Spirit Before
a Fall") or the joint product of a "musing Mount" and a "gloomy
Swamp" ("The Mountain and the Marsh"). These animadversions
turn upon nature and society, life in general, and a good deal of
follies in particular. In marshaling conflicting views, Lytton, no
less than other nineteenth-century authors of humorous tales
in prose and verse, is in full command of a bag of tricks to keep
the reader not only attentive and amused but committed to the
"right" view of the social and moral world as the only "natural"
one—a matter of common sense.[10] There is the intrusive narrator using exclamation marks and ironical interjections such as
"indeed!", "alas!", or "well-a-day!" (as when the eagle carrying the
tortoise, which is "thrilled [at] the contact of the great," predictably unclasps his claws) to create an attitude of smiling detachment where "folly" is all too evident. The inclusive "we" unites
narrator and narratee in a shared conviction of what greatness
and folly are, while apostrophe ("So aid me, Gentle Reader!")
creates an illusion of cooperation and mutual assent.

By establishing in his fiction a set of shared auctorial and
receptive positions, the author induces his readers to share with
him an ideology in the Althusserian sense, a number of seemingly self-evident images through which historically specific social relations are interpreted as natural, as "what goes without
saying."[11] Thus Lytton can quite casually do away with any claim
to the factual truth of his tales, and at the same time insist

on their verisimilitude—their homology with what everybody
accepts as generally true and morally right in the world of man,
the "fabulous" substructure of reality:

> ... But such tales as these
> May serve for morals, if their readers please,
> To all those fabulous things that so confound us
> By really happening in the world around us.

"Fabulous" is, of course, a pun. These lines suggest in a playful
way that the core of reality may well be fable (a fact that might
confound more skeptical minds) and that telling fables qualifies
as a form of realism. In 1874, of course, realism had been a
bone of contention in criticism for at least two decades. Lytton's
phrase elegantly conflates an apologia for fable writing with the
widespread commitment to what Walter Scott had already
termed "the art of copying from nature as she really exists."[12]
As a matter of fact, "if the readers please," there need not be any
tension between the two—provided one lets one's lofty images
preform and interpret the realities of one's world. And this is
just what Lytton's texts suggest.

In fable lore, this preformation and interpretation is largely
a linguistic one, a semantics implying unquestionable hierar-
chies of values. A seemingly "natural" code of values engages the
reader's sympathies for the eagle and against the tortoise, for
the stag and against the mole or the beetle, for the swan and
("naturally"!) against the pig.[13] It is this code that makes the
reader delight in a delicately coloured butterfly, image of beauty
(who ever heard of a crippled one?), and the smiling sun (never,
in our latitudes, thought of as, say, haughty or complacent) and
hate the destructive tempest. Moreover it incorporates value implications that English, like other languages, has fixed in conventional metaphors: "Minds ... whose natural home is high"—
like mountain summits—look down on "low natures" like
swamps. These preinterpreted images form nets of interrelated
codings: eagles soar high in a movement toward the transcendent, whereas the mole burrows in the dark. The stag majesti-
cally lifts his antlers as love "lifts" hearts to courage.

Such metaphorical precodings, in their turn, can easily (and
commonsensically) be extended to social groups with satirical
effect. In Lytton's *Fables* this social allegorizing is sometimes
made explicit in the epimythion. A commitment to real estate

(a connotation of the eagle's "natural home") justifies a derisive
aside on economic adventuring:[14]

> ...'Tis the way
> Of all industrial speculators.

More frequently, though, the reader has to infer the social allegory from features of the characters' speech. Not that it would
be difficult, for example, to recognize the obvious slight on (petit
bourgeois) evangelical self-improvement in the mole's aspiration
to the eagle's grandeur:

> "... By merit
> And painful perseverance, I,
> Tho' lowly born, may haply raise
> My humble self."

("A Tragedy of Errors", as the poem's subtitle indicates.) The
Master Piston of a ship's steam engine (to return to a text already
mentioned in our survey of satires) gives away his social position
in another discourse characteristic of the years around 1870:[15]

> "Privilege, Patronage, Compromise too,
> Down with them all, and let Labour be free!"

This stinging indictment of "Privilege, Patronage, filching the
name of Protection" is unfortunately directed against, of all
things, "that slippery, drivelling, intriguing Oil":

> "... this furtive Official Jack ... patting us all on the back,
> ... this lazy lord,
> Who affects, out of friendship, to take (our interests) in hand
> In convenient cant about compromise."

Those were the years when trade unionism began to emerge,
and terms like patronage and protection, compromise and con-
ciliation were opprobrium for the more radical advocates of
working-class rights. Lytton's sarcasm in thus confronting his
readers with a collection of subversive jargon could not easily
be missed. Probably it came as a surprise to no one that the
ship's engine, no longer oiled and greased, should run hot, and
the ship burst asunder.

At the other extreme in the hierarchy of precoded images,
which constitute a bond between poet and reader and construct

reality in this brand of realism,[16] we find praise of the poet's
"strength to be alone." Interpreting voluntary isolation as a heroic act that signals superiority, this suggests, in the linguistic
and rhetorical coding discussed, "eagle discourse" (cf. Wordsworth in *The Borderers*: "Solitude!—The Eagle lives in solitude").[17] In another Wordsworthian conception, of course, the
poetic genius, more passively, is known to possess "a more than
usual organic sensibility"[18] developed in meditative seclusion.
Thus in a two-layered allusion to solitude, Lytton calls up the
romantic sage as his authority on poetry—only (unconsciously?)
to reveal in the act his own following up of forms in an openly
didactic genre as far from either strong or visionary:

> The poet's form is to his followers known.
> The poet's secret is the poet's own.
> 'Tis born and buried in the poet's soul:
> Passion its prelude, solitude its goal.

It was late in the day of Romanticism, and in the 1870s, this
blend of mysticism and self-depreciation would itself have been
a signal of values shared by 'poet' and reader, like the admission
that in your "talk in verse" you may have stated the obvious once
too often. Thus in "The Mountain and the Marsh," a "venerable
Mount ... in wandering reverie" finds only scant attention to
his words, and the narrative invokes absolution for its own
occasional tedium as well as for the reader's understandable
tiredness:

> ... pausing for an answer, he perceived
> The water had been all this while asleep.
> Sleep, and good dreams be thine! There are sins worse
> Than too much talk in unregarded verse.

Conflicting Attitudes

Apart from gently directing the reader, all these devices—verbal
play and pastiche, allusions to a shared cultural heritage, insinu-
ating narrative strategies, and linguistic maneuvres in the field
of common sense—have the additional effect of constituting a
more or less clearly defined author image. This is the voice of a
gentleman, a conservative man of letters, probably of the landed
gentry, slightly supercilious, sarcastic, imperturbable, and at

home in the world as it is. Producing "talk in verse" rather than
poetry, his detachment embraces a mocking attitude, equally
"commonsensical," toward the philosophers' (and occasionally
his own) attempts to make sense of the world.

One would like to think that it was in a spirit of mild irony
that the narrator presented "ancient" Renard's rather mawkish
pantheism—"he lives in each living creature, / (Man, beast, bird,
blossom, and tree)" in the introductory section of the *Fables*.
More obviously the optimistic visions of Lytton's own more ponderous fables and reveries are occasionally undercut by
counterfables in light verse. As regards the Romantic heritage,
pantheism and the poetic afflatus—"the secret" (as just quoted)
"born and buried in the poet's soul"—, let us listen to a philosophizing windmill:

> "Thro' all my being, I know not how,
> But I feel the mystic impulse run
> Which mingles my life (this much I know)
> With the life of the mighty world. The sun,
> The moon, and stars, and the land, and seas,—
> In all does the Spirit of Nature lurk.
> He liveth in all, and he liveth in me . . .
> The voice is his, and the vision mine."

Sarcastically, however, the narrator identifies what actually
moves the mill:

> He may have o'ervalued his work and vocation,
> But philosophy often ends only in wind.

In "Teleology" a speculative nettle reflects on "The happiness of
nettles" in the jargon of Deism:

> How admirably organised is all
> This wondrous world! whose aspect everywhere
> Reveals to reverend thought, in great and small,
> Contrivance order'd with consummate care.

Crushed by a black slab of stone, however, the nettle's "crusht
philosophy, collapsing, miss(es) / Benignant purpose in the
blow" and immediately turns Darwinist:

> "Blind Chance it is! and since blind Chance obeys
> No guiding law". . .
> . . . the nettle died.

To the amusement of the dilettante, scientific no less than philosophical pride comes before (or, in this case, after) the fall, that
is, the crushed nettle marks in the slab of "carboniferous schist
... the impress of a plant of perisht centuries" and ("semper
vivens!") takes it for a fitting epitaph on its own destiny. Thus
science joins philosophy in a Vanity Fair of exempla where most
of the contemporary discourses can be bought quite cheaply.

However, there are (as indicated above) streaks of darker color
in this canvas of common sense and detachment, and it is these
that Stevenson, in his anatomy of the post-Darwinian "metaphysical" fable, was particularly concerned to bring out.

Thus to take but two instances, in the ironically titled "Monu-
mentum Aere Perennius," the narrator's eulogy of the poet's
high and solemn art is countered by mistrust of its truthfulness
and by skepticism as to its permanence. Smoke, it turns out, is
all that remains of man's achievements. Distressingly it is smoke
from a "soap-boiling manufactory" standing on the spot where
once a statue—apparently an "eternal monument"—honored a
poet whose works had, in their day, seemed eternal monuments
in celebrating heroic actions of the past—or rather, in truth,
thousandfold slaughter, oppression, and "tower and town tum-
bled in smoky ashes." In the narrator's disillusioned view, vulgarity in life has its counterpart in gross (and possibly
deliberate) misrepresentation in art. The implication seems to
be that things "really happening" may be far from "fabulous" (to
invert the earlier quotation). Thus, quite consistently, he ends
by assuming that the cycle of transience and futility, epitomized
in the permanence of dust and smoke, will finally include his
own narrative, "this narration," as well.

It was the pessimism of texts like this one which caused Stevenson's remark, in his review of 1874, about "truths that are a
matter of bitter concern." The fable, though, which (as initially
mentioned) he claimed made "the reader's indignation very
white-hot against someone," was an even more sombre tale, "The
Horse and the Fly," toward the end of the second book of Lytton's
collection. Here an act of maternal love (a horsefly stinging a
coach horse in the nose to deposit its eggs)[19] leads to most gruesome consequences, the death of the coachman, of a young cou-
ple, and a child. "Alas, what sufferings from a single cause,"

> Maternal Love, then, must we call
> Sole author of these mischiefs all?
> If so (at least on moral ground

Which some folks hold the only sound)
Methinks 'tis easier (search and try them)
To make laws than to justify them.

This is, obviously, Milton's famous project *à rebours*. The fabulist not only suggests a reduction of faith to morals (which was quite acceptable to many Victorians), but, in the name of morality, a repudiation of faith. For Stevenson this set the scene for the post-Darwinian fable of bitter truths—though Darwin would hardly seem the authority on which to base white-hot anger against one's creator (or his adversary). Anyway Lytton's fable collection contains, mainly in its later part, strange fits of skepticism and despair that do not quite match his carefully constructed author persona of calm common sense—allusive, mocking, and, one would like to think, ready to admit that his statesmanship might, after all, surpass his poetic craftsmanship.

Not surprisingly this evidence of conflicting authorial attitudes has its analogue in some rather intriguing *Fables in Song* themselves, which do not conform to the model of linguistic precodings and their commonsensical social interpretations under which the majority of the texts have been subsumed so far. However this is no longer a matter of paraphrasable content but of semantic and semiotic complexity. Only detailed attention to a specific text can show how words may multiply their meanings and plots submit to different decodings of their "truth." Thus the following chapter is exclusively concerned with one of Lytton's fables. It will be shown that, rather than having meaning, it invites an "oscillation," a moving back and forth between incompatible and mutually subversive readings, a self-deconstruction that prohibits any attribution of a strait noncontradictory message.

Lord Lytton's *Fables in Song* (II): Semiotic Model and Individual Text

Levels of Verisimilitude

A fable is a short piece of fiction, "one of the smallest of 'small' literary forms" (Needler), originally one of the Simple Forms (or, more pertinently, Primary Forms), that were defined as such by André Jolles in 1929.[1] Fables are told to convey truths concerning invariants of human behavior. They focus on what may be pragmatically favorable and profitable in concrete situations—the way they differ, in consequence, from emblems and emblematic tales has been mentioned in chapter 3. Following a pattern that, since the sixth century B.C., seems to have been connected with the name of the Phrygian slave Aesop, their prevailing attitude is one of skepticism, occasionally even cynicism—one thinks of La Fontaine's swallow, mentioned earlier, who demonstrates that those who are clever and strong are favored by Jupiter. Fables have promythia or, more frequently, epimythia, or morals, which are by no means their only meaning but part of a multileveled semiotic structure.[2]

This structure consists of different classes of signs and of corresponding kinds of verisimilitude—of what is accepted for each class of signs as plausible and "true to nature." What fables "mean" may best be conceived as the interplay of these plausibilities, combined with a mimetic and (optionally) axiological interpretation: "This is the way it is" and (think of the lobsters in Northcote or the crabs in Crane) "since this is the way it is let us help to keep it this way"—or, alternatively, "let us work for change."

This raises the problem of mimesis. In a way fables are certainly a-mimetic: "Only sentimental animal lovers believe that beasts are capable of moral actions" (Bausinger).[3] The basic sign vehicles are frequently (though by no means always) animals, plants, or inanimate things, which are presented as capable of speaking and acting rationally and (im)morally. This is obviously a long way from everyday experience and from the assumptions based on this experience. In fables spiders can complain to Jupiter, and butterflies are able to argue with the sun. Paradoxically what common sense would shrug off with a smile is here used to teach common sense in a very effective way, wooing the reader into a mixed attitude of amusement, reflection, and assent.

This is because, on the reader's side, the fable's feints of truth depend on decoding and deciphering.[4] In decoding, the reader fits the agents into culture-specific codes where they are tied to a fairly stable set of characteristics and values that constitute their verisimilitude: "The wolf is cruel and cowardly, the fox, wily, the bees, infinitely busy" (Bausinger). This decoding is evidently of several kinds. First empirical codes determine what we believe our sense experience confirms about the agents: the beauty, frailty, fragility, and zig-zag movements of butterflies, the scorching heat of the sun. To see that such knowledge is no more than a code that varies in time, between social groups, and between levels of education, the reader is reminded of Elizabeth Sandham on bees "gathering wax." The Rev. Ingram Cobbin, writing about the 'expectations' of indolent drones, stressed that he wrote about "the real habits of the animals."[5]

Second, moral codes determine the protagonists' characters often through the linguistic stereotypes based on metaphor that were discussed in the last chapter. Surely bookworms cannot be other than erudite. Butterflies are "volatile," thus fickle, flutter about, and are fond of sweet things, thus vain, conceited, idle, and promiscuous. And the sun, at least for white Anglo-Saxon bookworms, is strong and glorious, thus majestic. These are as fine examples as any of empirical and moral coding:

> A butterfly, with fine painted wings, flew from flower to flower, and seemed to wish everyone to admire its beauty. "You rove from flower to flower all the long summer day; pray, Madam Butterfly, when do you find time for work?"

> > "Ha, Ha! I know of nought to beat
> > The tiny butterfly's conceit."[6]

Furthermore, codes that are historically variable relate groups of animals in identical plot roles with specific professions or social positions. Thus in the Middle Ages, "preachy Chantecler" represented the priest, and the fox generally "friar, or bishop" (Henderson).[7] In 1874 Lytton's eagle is still clearly lord of his demesne, whereas the mole shows the code's variability to embrace more recent socioreligious developments. Consequently the seeming truth of the fable's agents and their actions depends on the variable social and moral codings of the world of man. Where diligence and earnestness come together in Protestant work ethics, the busy bees are "naturally" appealed to in matters of "The Law of Authority and Obedience" (as in Margaret Gatty's *Fables from Nature*), while fin-de-siècle aestheticism feels free to poke fun gently at their pomposity: "'They are wise and know the secrets of life . . .' But the rose detested the bees") ("The Rosebud").[8] Thus, as Howard Needler puts it, "unlike larger literary genres, which create an order of their own through their poetic fictions, fable presupposes an order (which will) . . . differ in accordance with the cultural assumptions of the writer."

To conclude, Needler's study proposes an additional, and possibly controversial, semiotic property of the fable. In his analysis, "in almost any animal fable . . . the presumed order is viewed from different perspectives":

> One of these is the view of an idealized morality that respects honesty and innocence, demands succor for the weak and needy, shows gratitude where thanks are due, pays debts and reciprocates kindnesses, and so on. The other view is of a dog-eat-dog world characterized by greed, exploitation, ingratitude, viciousness, pitilessness, and so on. In a typical fable both perspectives are present . . .
>
> For this reason fable is an unusually marginal form . . . its essence resides in the capture of a scene at a critical juncture, where its two faces are both clearly visible.

Because of this intrinsic doubleness of perspective, the moral, for Needler, is "always implicit in the body of the fable . . . and may even be . . . identical with the fable"[9]—not, that is, with its epimythion.

The reader may well feel that this claim is too general. But I would suggest that it was this possibility of a multiple, and finally ambiguous, attribution of meaning that made the production of original fables, such as the *Fables in Song,* anything but a dull and mechanical affair. Lytton seems to have been well aware that the modern fable writer could either, as it were, play variations on the commonplace codes—or reshuffle, and ambiguously redefine, their signifiers.

He could, that is, fit new sign vehicles into the established code positions—let a mole compare himself with an eagle, as Aesop's mouse vies with a lion. That meant retelling a moral tale, and—on an additional level of verisimilitude, that of socially acceptable distortion—having a satirical fling at contemporary follies. Or he could play havoc with the old codes, explode cultural stereotypes, and invent new fables in an essentially "marginal" form, with "endlessly varied intersections" of the two "different perspectives" of ideal and "greed, exploitation, ingratitude, viciousness, pitilessness, and so on."[10]

He might, for instance, imagine a butterfly as crippled, "an abortion / Doomed from its birth to suffering and distortion,"[11] or the sun as envious of the disabled insect. Now on the reader's side, *deciphering* would have to take over from *decoding*—an attempt to attest "meaning" to a tale that has done away with evident coded content. A last type of verisimilitude would have to be established rather than taken for granted. This plausibility would draw its strength from collective images and myths, "ideologies," which, though largely unconscious, are powerful tools in people's attempts to "make sense" of their lives and justify their actions—or possibly, from the violation of these images and myths. Crippled beauty and a splendour that is visibly tainted might emblematize, for different readers, the shortcomings of a postlapsarian world, insufficient caring in modern society, the corruptions under capitalism, a satire on Post-Impressionist painting, or (on a metalevel) an attempt to replace coded fables by noncoded ones. When, in a strongly coded literary genre, the signifiers are stripped of their signifieds, signification is replaced by *dissémination,* parables become anything but pointers to moral truths, and the epimythion, Stevenson's "succinct formula," has to give way to a *paramythion,* an interpretative text waiting to be written.

The hypothetical images in the preceding paragraphs were taken from one of Lord Lytton's fables, "Questionable Consolation." An analysis of this text reveals signals that suggest the adequacy of a nondecoding reading. In fact, this fable "has nothing to say of the morally well-ordered world in its own right, or of the corrupted order of tyrants and exploiters in its own right; it finds its proper interests in the manifold and endlessly varied intersections of these two."[12] The following study of "Questionable Consolation" will show that Needler's metaphor of intersection had better be replaced by that of oscillation, a moving back and forth, of incompatible and mutually subversive readings, a self-deconstruction that prohibits any attribution of a univocal, noncontradictory message.[13]

QUESTIONABLE FABULATION

"Questionable Consolation" introduces the reader to the crippled butterfly and to the sun as its magnificent (and rather arrogant) opponent. Witness the insect,

> One wing unfinisht, and misshapen one ...
> The piteous pivot of his own distress,
> Aye with self-torturing unsteadiness
> About himself he turn'd; and found no aid.[14]

This initial description, if untrue to metaphorical stereotype, is, however, certainly true (i.e., plausible) relative to sociopsychological verisimilitude. Severe disfigurement leads to distress, breeds self-torture, and makes one cry for help. Thus the fable binds its readers (particularly if we take account of the Victorians' high esteem for charity) to a response of pity ("piteous") and goodwill ("aid"). At the outset this response appears to be part of the narrated world as well. The "dying sun" takes up the creature's wish "to disappear—go down—go by—/ Sink out of life" and, to console it, points to its own immediate fate: "Mourn not! I even, I, the sun go down, / Sink, and drop into darkness." Then satisfied that his departure is universally regretted and rejoicing at the light and force he, one of "the happy," has been able to give to the world, "in pompous purple" he passes: "Thus suns go down."

In these words of the narrator, irony quickly displaces what, for an instant, may have suggested an implied approval of the sun's friendly disposition. This move is reflected in the narrated universe as well, and with a vengeance. Not surprisingly the butterfly has only disdain for the sun's complacency:

> The boastful orb's last glories, lingering,
> That cripple smote. "Go, glories! tell your king,"
> Smiling he said, "go, him that sent you tell,
> Not all so wretched as I deemed was I.
> Since I have seen how suns go down, thereby
> School'd have I been to know, and value well,
> What they, the happy,—they that have it not,—
> Would fain filch even from a wretch's lot,

The grandeur of its utter desolation."
All glowing with rebuke and shamed vexation
The braggart sun's resentful blushes burst.
As o'er the deep, whose surface, and no more,
His glory gilt, he, slowly sinking, bore
This knowledge gain'd: That Misery at her worst
Hath one poor grace of tragic interest
Proud Pleasure vainly envies at his best.

These are the last lines of the text, and the position that the reader is impelled to adopt seems clear. Pride goes before a fall (or sinking), "the happy," never having tasted despair, may not be so very happy (or at least so full of "grandeur") after all. Apparently decoding the fable as a variation on familiar themes provides a good deal of moral plausibility—this is, after all, the case of La Fontaine's fox and crow over again, with a creature of superior acumen perceiving complacency as essentially vulnerable and, by its skill in rhetoric, going one better. This reading suits Theo Elm's hypothesis[15] concerning parabolic structure: the reader is moved to reconsider and revise commonplace concepts, arriving at more deeply considered views.

Thus the revision suggested would seem to be a twofold one, concerning ready-made (coded) images and stereotypes of human relationships. As for the latter, social implications below the obvious ones are as easy to see here as in Lytton's fables summarized above: "Questionable Consolation" reveals an additional touch of satirical verisimilitude, if, considering the author's aristocratic name, the fable is read as a satire on the self-satisfaction of the ruling classes—a complacency too easily bought by acts of charity, if not by mere cant. The fable foregrounds its own process of reader reorientation in the butterfly's words "school'd have I been" and the sun's admission of "knowledge gained."

Or does it? Quite possibly to some readers it may seem that the fable doth protest too much. Upgrading Misery in the face of Proud Pleasure as having its own compensations in "grandeur of desolation" and in a "grace of tragic interest" is, after all, nothing but another piece of self-satisfaction easily bought. The title "Questionable Consolation" seems to take account of this. Its surface meaning certainly turns against the "schooling" (or self-delusion) of the butterfly. But it may likewise undercut precisely this latter brand of complacency, the sun's "knowledge gained," shame-faced, it is true, but not altogether unwelcome as a consolation in the face of suffering and injustice.

Finally on a further level of meaning, moral criticism, and satire, as "knowledge gained" through interpretative movements, may themselves be shown up as rather questionable delusions about a text that is less a correction of commonplaces than a denunciation of incontrovertible readings. Ambiguating certain thematic signifiers—sign-expressions available for multiple recontextualization—the text, no longer a parable in any conventional sense, effects their circulation around various centers, one of which may be contempt or cynicism rather than schooling and knowledge.

This may be said to create its own plausibility or truth in opposition to what is generally believed to be true, normal, and right in the world of man. On the text's premises, it seems plausible that man is eager to humiliate his fellow creatures and—in the image of the butterfly—to gloat over this humiliation, to the last gasp, regardless of his own anguish and agony. Thus the insect, in the end, deems itself "not all so wretched," "smil(ing)" in its own brand of Proud Pleasure—"blemisht," a "wretch," "Misery at her worst" in more than one meaning of the words, unhappy and trying to cause unhappiness in its turn. Refuting its own claim of "the grandeur of its utter desolation," the butterfly proves what the text ironically (and against the meaning of the sun's concession) calls a "*poor* grace of tragic interest." There is, indeed, in the sun as in its antagonist, very little grandeur and even less grace. The edifying ideas of consolation and compensation (if questionable) turn into their sarcastic distortion, a lashing out against general vulgarity, against *poor grace* as a universal loss of dignity and self-respect. Contempt takes the place of moralizing. The speaker's stance approximates to that of an impeccable social superiority and culture that sees fit to denounce everything that comes into sight, misery as evil and "pompous purple" (albeit that of the sun) as *nouveau riche,*— which, after all, is not a far cry from the persona we deduced earlier from the paraphrasable content of other fables.

A text like this certainly demands the reader's activity—his or her working out of alternative meanings which depend on and relativize each other or even cancel each other out. For arguably, what we, again rather rashly, called its final level of meaning had better, in the inhumanity of its general contempt, take its clue from the sun and submit to the "rebuke" of insufficient compassion—of a failure, that is, to discover, not the insect's but the fable's "grace of tragic interest." On the other hand (or rather on one more footing), sympathy with the cripple "defrauded / Of what mere life makes capable of joy" and with its more pitiable than questionable consolation would, as a sentimental misreading, easily come under the barrage of all three readings which claim their authority from the title word "questionable."

These oscillations of meaning (which do not, as pluralists would wish, mutually enrich each other) may be compared to reversal techniques in picture puzzles like the rabbit-duck phenomenon dear to psychologists and art historians. From the visual arts one could mention the well-known chalk drawing *Grave* (1917) by Otto Dix. Here, while a dead soldier's body seems already to have become one with Great Nature (another image of questionable consolation and, perhaps, compensation), in a sarcastic perspective, 'nature' may appear as nothing but a deceptive coating spread over the corpse that stays on as an ineffaceable symbol of the horror and futility of war. This phenomenon has recently attracted attention in literary studies as well. In his essay "Either/Or: Responding to *Henry V*" (1981), Norman Rabkin has given an influential interpretation of Shakespeare's history play that is based on Gombrich, reading the play as "constructed so that readers can and must interpret it alternately as either 'rabbit' or 'duck,' a condemnation or a celebration of war."[16] Likewise what in Lytton's fable may be presumed to be a center of meaning is never more than a point that may just as well belong to the arcs of other circles.

A short summarizing statement of the assumptions that have directed the arrangement of the material in chapter 4 (on prose fables down to Stevenson) and in this chapter—their gradual advance toward instances of indeterminacy—may be in place. Theo Elm's theory of the (premodern) parabolic fable as a structure that gently propels its reader through positions of limited comprehension ("Positionen der Uneinsichtigkeit") toward a mature understanding ("ein Ort erkenntnisbringender Reflexion") presupposes one correct reading ("Erkenntnis") of this structure. Developed within the Wirkungsästhetik of the School of Constance, this assumption is a late offspring of structuralism. Attending, on the other hand, to the slippery character of language which may extend even to the signifieds of seemingly robust and reliable signifiers like "home," "happy," "conclusive," "good" and "bad," "superstition" (in Stevenson) or "questionable" and "consolation" (in Lytton), recent criticism prefers the metaphor of deconstruction to that of structure[17] and may take the liberty of pointing even to the paragon of didacticism, the fable, as a verbal space where various collocations of signifiers produce different, equally valid, and mutually subversive meanings.[18]

7

Walter Crane's *The Baby's Own Aesop*— Visual Countertexts in a Victorian Picture Book

A GAME FOR TWO

CHILDREN, it is true, are not just a smaller version of adults, but adults occasionally love to act as if they were still children. Thus there are many children's books whose subtlety must be beyond the capacities of the young while their authors are likely to have rejoiced at their chance to dabble in nonsense covering deeper meaning. In particular this constellation may have produced many of those picture books which, by means of their sophisticated illustrations and allusive texts, appeal first and foremost to adult readers.

The subject of this chapter is one of them. It was created by Walter Crane and William J. Linton in 1887 and bore the title *The Baby's Own Aesop*—at first sight a picture book for very small children.[1] However, the title proves misleading. In addition to various linguistic games, the work contains elaborate and allusive wood engravings reproduced in what was then the most advanced technique of color printing. At the time of its publication, the book was described as an "aesthetic little quarto"— clearly an allusion to the Aesthetic Craze of the 1870s and 1880s. More than a century later, its texts and pictures are still a pure delight.

In the present context, however, the focus of interest is semiotic rather than aesthetic. Crane's and Linton's book invites inquiries as to the nature of illustration. The pictures in *The Baby's Own Aesop* greatly exceed a mere doubling of the narratives. They amount to a subtle creation of visual "countertexts." To some extent these counterplots and their references are suggested by an inversion of the time-honored conventions of the

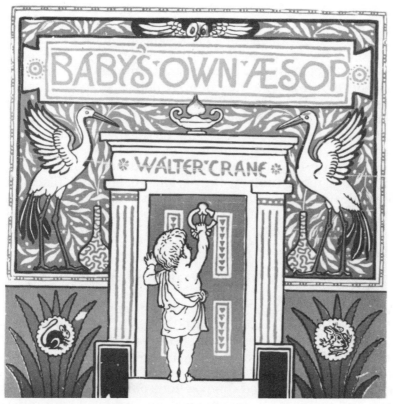

Walter Crane, *The Baby's Own Aesop* (cover)

emblematic fable, which have been discussed at an earlier point as one of the models of nineteenth-century fables in verse.[2] Thus after some introductory remarks on the character of the book and its genesis, I will first give an account of this semiotic transformation—semiotic in that it involves a new relationship between text and image combined with a change in the relative semantic loads of the two media—and then proceed to study what I would like to call the book's *visual rhetoric of tropes and schemes*. Traditionally *trope,* or "figure of sense," is the term for words used in a way that effects a conspicuous change in their standard meaning. *Scheme,* or "figure of arrangement," is the term for words in a particular order that may affect their meaning as well. My assumptions are thus based on principles of describing linguistic devices. No doubt it would be more correct to replace the term *rhetoric* with some neologism like *emphatics* (from gr. *em-* and *phainain-*, to show), but *visual rhetoric* preserves more of the shape of my argument.[3]

As in rhetoric, readers may derive additional significance from the tropes and schemes of a book's visual rhetoric—what might be called its *depicting* (or, to quote the book's title page, its "pointing pictorially") as opposed to its mimetic *picturing*. (Conversely, Arthur Kelly's "Rosebud," which lacks such visual evocativeness, was described on its title page as "pictured by Walter Crane."[4]) Domains of this additional significance can be determined by means of cultural contexts. In the case of Crane's picture book, two evident contexts of the 1880s and 1890s were the playfully derisive antibourgeois attitudes of aestheticism and, more momentously, the serious, combative, placard-style simplifications of socialism (for which Crane in 1895 designed his *Cartoons for the Cause*). This aspect of possible reference will be discussed later in this chapter.

THE ORIGIN OF *THE BABY'S OWN AESOP*

Walter Crane (1845–1915) was an illustrator of books and magazines, a successful designer of fabrics and wallpapers, and—to his chagrin, much less successfully—a painter. Between 1865 and 1906, he created about fifty colored picture books (among them about thirty toy books for very small children), many of which are sophisticated compositions of binding, end leaf paper, text, and pictures. As a young man he had been apprenticed to William Linton (1812–97), one of the nineteenth-century masters of wood engraving. In 1887 Linton suggested they cooperate on an illustrated picture book and sent him 66 five-line stanzas, each of which retold one of Aesop's fables.[5]

The stanzas had a form that later, around the end of the century, was to acquire notoriety as the limerick.[6] Edward Lear (1818–88)—an amiable and eccentric genius, an artist who had won recognition as John Gould's illustrator for his *Birds of Europe*—had made this playful form of nonsensical rhyming the talk of the town with the third edition of his *Book of Nonsense* in 1861. For months on end, the people of London vied with one another in rhyming.

Edward Lear's "learicks" (as they might be called to emphasize their special character) were different from limericks as we know them today. For one thing they rarely made use of phonetic ambiguities and witty spellings. Moreover they were in no way "off-color." On the other hand they were much more nonsensical. Lear's verses related stories of characters in exotic places

Edward Lear, "There Was an Old Man with a Nose"

whose strange afflictions and odd whims seemed more than far-fetched. The old men and young ladies served, as it were, exclusively the Rule of Rhyme, as in the case of the remarkable man whose nose was too long:

> There was an Old Man with a nose.
> Who said, "If you choose to suppose
>   That my nose is too long,
>   You are certainly wrong!"
> That remarkable man with a nose.[7]

Linton's Aesopian stanzas clearly followed this model and contributed to the plethora of limericks avant la lettre. One of his verses dealt in its turn with a part of the body that was much too long. In Aesop this was the throat or "throttle" of a crane, which Linton used to get in a joking dig at his younger colleague, who seems to have been no contemner of the bottle:

> You have heard how Sir Fox treated Crane:
> With soup in a plate. When again
>   They dined, a long bottle
>   Just suited Crane's throttle;
> And Sir Fox licked the outside in vain
> THERE ARE GAMES THAT TWO CAN PLAY AT

Obviously the last line, the epimythion, is ambiguous. It suggests that in some games one may meet one's match. But the game that two can play at probably also refers to the book project

Walter Crane, "The Fox & the Crane" from *The Baby's Own Aesop*

proposed by Linton. As we know he met his match; Crane accepted his suggestion. The outcome was one of the most charming picture books of Victorian England.

THE ARTISTS AND SOME CONTEXTS OF THE BOOK'S PRODUCTION

In conferring an aristocratic title upon Sir Fox, penny-pinching and hypocritical, Linton injected into Aesop a dash of social criticism—an insider joke between two artists close to the Socialist Movement, which was gaining momentum at the time.

In the first half of the century, Linton had been a member of the Chartists, who fought for the extension of basic political rights in England—for universal male (though not female) suffrage as well as for secret ballot, the payment of members of Parliament, annual parliamentary elections, and equal electoral districts. Between 1837 and 1848, such extreme and, as it appeared at the time, rebellious demands found support above all in the working classes, which led to general unrest and violent revolts. To promote Chartist ideas, Linton had put the little money he owned into magazines that he illustrated himself. A friend of Mazzini, he had delivered to the Parisian revolutionaries of 1848 an official address from the London Working Men's Association. Among Linton's writings are a defense of the Paris Commune and a biography of Thomas Paine, the author of the *Rights of Man*.[8]

Walter Crane, his former apprentice, later drifted into the Morris circle. From 1885 he was a member of Morris's Socialist League. He gave lectures at meetings of the Fabian Society (which counted Shaw and Wells among its members) and created numerous designs for political placards and flags. Socialist magazines like *Justice* and *The Commonweal* published allegories from his pen, which were collected in 1896 as *Cartoons for the Cause*.[9]

By 1876 Crane had already designed about thirty toy books, which were published by Routledge and sold at the price of sixpence or a shilling. They contained illustrations of children's rhymes, fairy tales, and plain stories of everyday life. They sported color plates, which, with their fanciful treatment of costumes and interiors, possessed much charm. It is easy to detect in them the influence of Renaissance painting, as well as that of Japanese color prints, which were becoming popular in those years. With the creation of these toy books, Crane fathered a line of picture books, which, while suitable for small children, were conceived as beautiful things in their own right. The artist was destined to become "the academic of the nursery," as P. G. Konody called him in 1902. Crane, who had seen many of his paintings rejected by the Royal Academy, did not particularly appreciate the term.

The Baby's Own Aesop was published in 1887, the third in a series of three Christmas books that were of particularly exquisite design, following *The Baby's Opera* (1877) and *The Baby's Bouquet* (1878), which contained illustrations and musical settings of English and Continental children's rhymes. At five shillings the books in this series were rather expensive—a venture for the publishers which, however, soon proved worthwhile. In a short time their success brought rivals like Kate Greenaway and Randolph Caldecott to the scene.

Even among these more sumptuously illustrated books, the *Aesop* of 1887 was the first to appeal primarily to adult readers due to its highly allusive illustrations and the complexity of its linguistic games. At the same time, the style of the illustrations was downright avant-garde. It was (in present-day terms) early art nouveau, owing much of its inspiration to the graphic work of William Blake, which had recently been made accessible to a wider public in the second edition of Gilchrist's *Life of Blake* (1880). The plates of the first edition had been prepared by Linton at the time when Crane was his apprentice. The illustrations document similarities of design—in the flowing, swirling pattern derived from plants including a suggestion of petals or leaves—between one of the prints in Blake's *Europe* (1794), as reprinted by Gilchrist, and a plate from Crane's *Aesop*.[10]

The refinement of delicate hues in Crane's "aesthetic little quarto" proved that the artist was also an experienced watercolorist. However the exquisite coloring was equally due to new technical developments. Since 1865 the printer and artist Edmund Evans had significantly enhanced the quality of reproducing colored wood engravings. The technical perfection he achieved, and his clever selection of the artists he contracted— Crane and, as already mentioned, Randolph Caldecott and Kate Greenaway—rapidly made the new genre of artistically designed colored picture books a stunning success with the public.[11]

LATE EMBLEMATICS

Crane's and Linton's *Aesop* is clearly related, in its motifs and in its pictorial elements, to emblem books and their pictorial tradition. In Crane's designs the tripartite emblematic structure of *pictura (symbolon), inscriptio (lemma),* and *subscriptio* is immediately obvious. Moreover if we juxtapose an emblem from, say Johann Mannich's *Sacra Emblemata* (1625)[12] and Crane's "King Log & King Stork," we recognize a remarkable similarity in the constellation of the divine hand, paper, sun, and the protagonist. Crane's picture may thus be read as a deliberate playing around with emblematic conventions. Comparing, however, Crane's imaginative late emblematics with the pictorial tradition that Hermann Tiemann has called "the emblematic form of the fable,"[13] we note two important differences.

The first distinction is the extreme paring down of the text to the five lines of Linton's limericks and their one-line morals. Let us consider, for the sake of comparison, two well-known works of the Renaissance emblematic tradition, *Fables du tres-ancien Esope, Phrygien* and *Hecatomgraphie* (Paris, printed by Denys Janot, 1542 and 1543). A print from the *Hecatomgraphie* has already been reproduced, with a discussion of its text, near the beginning of chapter 2.[14] In these collections of fables and emblems by the compiler Gilles Corrozet—both of which have an identical layout—the woodcut with *inscriptio* and a four-line epigram is followed, as Tiemann puts it, by "a full (recto) page with explanatory verses of different kinds," a rat's tail, as it were, of explanations and reflections. "In the sixteenth century these additions become . . . more and more diverse and comprehensive." According to Albrecht Schöne, the emblematic fable develops "towards a moralizing chap-book."[15] Mannich's baroque emblem (as the section given on p. 124 can only suggest) is itself followed by a long reflective poem which, in its turn, has a motto included in it. Because the emblematic *pictura* is meant to "picture" this text plainly and lucidly, it seems to depend on a fairly extensive verbal specification of what is shown and why it is shown.

Seen in this way, Crane and Linton would appear to have cut down the rules of the game by half. Edification is in no way on the agenda here. We read, one might say, an emblem book with no recto pages. The capitals of the inscriptions (DON'T HAVE KINGS! REASON FROM RESULTS) would seem to be all that is left to tell what this late emblematizing is about at all. Less to "point a moral," it appears, than to "adorn the tale," to nail it down (some of the inscriptions are actually on metal bands) to a moral or political slogan, one of a number of (as the title has it) "Portable Morals."

Thus among the verbal components, the tale moves to the center, reduced though it is to the five lines of a limerick. Quite consistently the position of the text shows an obvious deviation from the tradition of the emblematic fable. Linton's stanza is allotted the space traditionally reserved for the *pictura,* while the visual matter now *surrounds* the text and extends right to the picture's frame. Consider Crane's "The Ass & the Sick Lion," which shows his version of the same fable of the crafty lion that was discussed earlier in Corrozet's *Hecatomgraphie.* The spatial

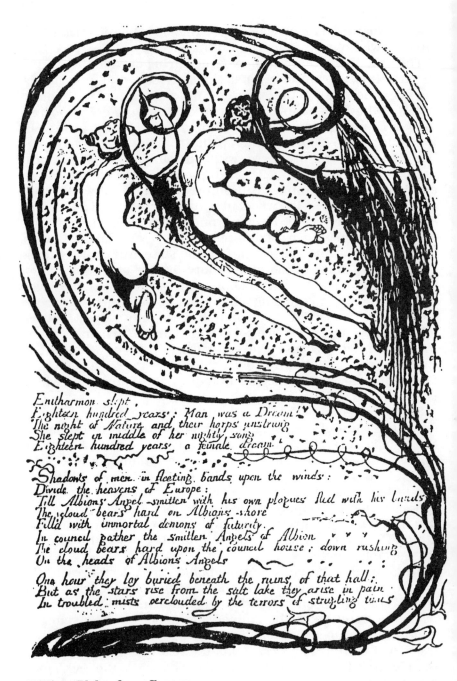

Enitharmon slept.
Eighteen hundred years: Man was a Dream!
The night of Nature and their harps unstrung
She slept in middle of her nightly song
Eighteen hundred years a female dream.

Shadows of men in fleeting bands upon the winds:
Divide the heavens of Europe:
Till Albions Angel smitten with his own plagues fled with his bands
The cloud bears hard on Albions shore
Filld with immortal demons of futurity.
In council gather the smitten Angels of Albion
The cloud bears hard upon the council house; down rushing
On the heads of Albions Angels

One hour they lay buried beneath the ruins of that hall:
But as the stars rise from the salt lake they arise in pain
In troubled mists oerclouded by the terrors of struggling times

William Blake, from *Europe*

THE COCK & THE PEARL

A ROOSTER, while scratching for grain, Found a Pearl. He just paused to explain That a jewel's no good To a fowl wanting food, And then kicked it aside with disdain.

"IF HE ASK BREAD WILL YE GIVE HIM A STONE?"

Walter Crane, "The Cock & the Pearl" from *The Baby's Own Aesop*

relationship between picture and text has been inverted. In all of the thirty plates of the book which treat a single fable, it is no longer the picture that receives interior framing but Linton's verse.

Iconically this is perfectly convincing. It fits the concise and invariable metric structure of the limericks, which allows for no proliferation, as well as their sophisticated linguistic "engraving." In the *Aesop,* the text, a mere stanza, chiseled, cameolike, is presented as an artifact, a silhouette of intertextual reminiscences—and occasionally, as will be seen, a site of reversals of meaning that can become as puzzling as those discussed earlier in one of Lytton's fables.

Clearly it has lost the function it had in the emblem books of the Renaissance, of elucidating, explaining, and interpreting the world. Instead in accordance with our thesis of a nonmimetic 'depicting' or 'pointing', the *Aesop* plates reveal a complex and ambivalent relationship between a verbal and a visual rhetoric, between punning and a significant order of visual components, such as J. Hillis Miller has claimed characterizes the illustration of literary texts in general:

> The relation between text and illustration is clearly reciprocal. Each refers to the other. Each illustrates the other, in a continual back and forth movement . . . Illustrations in a work of fiction displace the sign-referent relationship assumed in a mimetic reading and replace it by a complex and problematic reference between two radically different kinds of sign, the linguistic and the graphic.[16]

Mann. S. 25   **Sonne** *und Gottes Wort, davor ein Mann mit abgewendetem Kopf*

QUID, TUNE VENIRE RECUSAS?

Rom. II. v. IIII.

DOMINICA II. TRINITATIS, EVANG. LUC. 14. V. 16.

verstockter   Ivstitiae Solem stupidus spernit: nec habere
Unglaube   Literulam, ad coenam quae jubet ire, cupit.
          Aeternum si quis temnit, mundana requirens
          Tantum, hunc post obitum tristia fata manent.

Verachtung blind
Gnad nimmer findt.

IN der Figur ein Sonn man sicht /
Wie sie deß morgens frü außbricht:
Die zeigt vns Gottes Gütigkeit /
Die er vns in seim Wort anbeut /
Sie ist all morgen new behend /
Sein Güt hat nimmermehr kein end.
Auß der Wolck geht ein Hand herfür /
Die da ein Brieff weist von Papier /
Deß HERREN Wort zeigt der Brieff an /
Was er von vns will allen han.
Daß wir dasselb mit allen Ehrn
Fleissig solln lesn / vnd gern hörn.
Der Mann hie mit vmbkehrten Gsicht /
Der Menschen art vns schön bericht /
Die jmmerdar exorbitirt /
Vnd Gott in seim Wort reformirt:
Nur nach dem zeitlichen stets tracht /
Deß ewigen gar wenig acht /
Drumb muß er endlich beydes lassn /
Wenn er wird fahren seine Strassn.

Ps. 136, 8; Klage 3, 23; Gregor. M. ep. IV 40; Ps. 78, 1; Matth. 11, 9;
Luk. 7, 35

Johann Mannich, "Quid, Tune Venire Recusas?"

Text within the illustration:

KING LOG & KING STORK

THE FROGS prayed to
Jove for a king:
"Not a log, but a livelier
thing."
Jove sent them a Stork,
Who did royal work,
For he gobbled them up, did
their king.

DON'T HAVE KINGS

Walter Crane, "King Log & King Stork" from *The Baby's Own Aesop*

Replacing the world of emblematic texts, static, grounded in transcendence, a "truly universal web of relations and meanings,"[17] Crane's plates, interacting with Linton's limericks, create a "world of images" that may invite a world of imaginings. Here, then, is the place to go into the particulars of this rhetorically structured visual world, which, mainly through a semiotization of spatial relationships, suggests within the Aesopian contours a variety of contemporary attitudes, events, and political grievances.

THE RHETORIC OF DEPICTION (I): A PLAY OF SIGNIFIERS

Even a first glance at the cover of *The Baby's Own Aesop,* shown at the beginning of this chapter, indicates clearly how marked

Walter Crane, "The Ass & the Sick Lion" from *The Baby's Own Aesop*

were Crane's references to the ornamental art of Renaissance bookmaking with its decorative floral borders.[18] However in one of his plates, "Brother & Sister," borders and ledges become signifiers in their own right. Multiple framing creates mimetic as well as semiotic space, separating as well as juxtaposing the "twin children," while their father, crossing a doorstep toward "the girl," is set apart from "the brother" by heavy ornamental borders. Meander stripes on the curtain twice repeat the horizontal ledges of the picture frame, as do the metal bands above and below the text and the faintly antique molding that marks off the pedestal on which the young man sits. Likewise the vertical ledges of the frame are repeated within the picture several times, half of the folds of the old man's himation form vertical parallels, while a stela of Pallas Athena next to a doorpost gives the plate a threefold right-hand vertical boundary. Clearly antiquity and the rectilinear together suggest authority and rectitude, as univocal a message as that nailed down on the metal bar— "Handsome is as handsome does":

> Twin children: the Girl, she was plain;
> The Brother was handsome & vain;
>   "Let him brag of his looks,"
>   Father said; "mind your books!
> The best beauty is bred in the brain."
> HANDSOME IS AS HANDSOME DOES

There are some hints, however, that not all these rectangularities are to be read as straight as they appear at first sight. There may be irony, for example, in the right angle that is formed by the father's lifted forefinger and the scroll in his hand, because it suggests the sign of a cross and thus exorcism rather than warning. And with good reason, for while "the best beauty" that the fable teaches is one that sadly escapes picturing, the old man's gesture of pictorial pointing places emphasis on a kind of beauty flagrantly contrary to bourgeois notions of what is "good." In a way Crane's picture book, at this point, may claim the title *The Decadent's Own Aesop*.

As a matter of fact, Linton's text itself already has a great deal of trouble with rectitude. It is out of books, the wise old man says, that the best beauty is bred. The best mind certainly— Athena obviously nods agreement to the teachings of the Victorian sage Matthew Arnold, who found in literature "the best that has been thought and said." However, what the epimythion, speaking of "doing," makes of this text is not exactly conclusive. To say the least, it is extremely optimistic—implying that she who knows "the best" cannot help doing other people good. If so, is Linton, tongue in cheek, casting an ironic light on the idyllic family scenario so dear to the Victorians and on the notion that good breeding helps to develop a good heart?

This light, however, may fall from an entirely different source as well. Text and epimythion are exposed to a contest of ironies that appears difficult to settle. The stock phrase that Linton uses has been recorded, in texts of 1580 and 1600, as "Goodly is that goodly does" (Anthony Munday) and "He is proper that proper does" (Thomas Dekker). One *is* what one does. True, John Gay,

Anon., *Aesopus Moralisatus*

BROTHER & SISTER

TWIN children: The Girl,
        she was plain;
The Brother was handsome &
            vain;
" Let him brag of his looks,"
    Father said, mind your books!
The best beauty is bred in the brain"

HANDSOME IS AS HANDSOME DOES

Walter Crane, "Brother & Sister" from *The Baby's Own Aesop*

in 1713, writes, "He is handsome that handsome does," yet this
still preserves the old meaning: "handsome," in his day, meant
"easy to manipulate," "handy"—he is helpful that acts help-
fully.[19] It is only Linton's limerick that foregrounds the witty
effect which accrues from the shift in meaning of 'handsome'
to 'graceful' and 'beautiful'—the catachresis of a beauty outside
the aesthetic (or, conceivably, for at least some of the book's
readers the nonparadox of the Platonic *kalokagathia,* the unity
of the good and the beautiful). The socialist writer of sarcastic
limericks would hardly have failed to notice that what was really
at issue here was a highly questionable notion of the middle
classes: the conviction that a woman's beauty lay in her ability
to please male judgment by showing either grace or culture. If

the satiric stage here is apparently Vanity Fair, behind the curtain the Victorian marriage market looms large.

This blending of perspectives in Linton's text—deadpan or subtly inversive—is carried even further in Crane's design. Three years prior to Wilde's *The Picture of Dorian Gray*, a face that is effete and of marble pallor, beautifully framed in a mirror, seems to confront earnestness and philistinism with the exposed existence of the artist. For evidently "the Brother . . . handsome and vain," in circlet and robe resembling his sister, is not only a poet (could the lyrics on his lap be subversive learicks?), but a transvestite—framed as a picture within the picture, in front of gold ground arts and crafts tapestry, posing on a pedestal as a statue that seems to be a nasty parody of the statuelike old sage. His narcissism comes across as a confusingly ambivalent signifier. Removed from the bourgeois order of signs and "pictorially pointing" to a life of desire, it glides away from the "best beauty," unaffected "plainness" and naturalness, and seems to argue for the allurements of an assumedly better beauty.

THE RHETORIC OF DEPICTION (II): TROPES AND THEIR REFERENCE

Since at least the Middle Ages, Aesopian fables had easily admitted political subtexts.[20] Many of Linton's verses, too, have the epimythion THERE WERE POLITICIANS IN AESOP'S TIME invisibly written into them—a line that he affixes to the fable of the fox who, having been attacked by a swarm of mosquitoes, nevertheless bids them stay for fear that an even more hungry swarm might set upon him. In his pointed lines, more than once ("by Goad!") his puns reveal bitterness, if not sarcasm.

In the fable "The Wolf and the Lamb," for example, quibbling exposes the distortion of words as a dangerous instrument for manipulating others. As is well known, the lamb's response to a torrent of unjust reproaches from the hungry wolf is that it could not possibly have made the stream muddy since at the time in question it was not even born. This, however, does not impress the wolf in the least:

> Answered Wolf—"then 'twas Ewe—
> Ewe or lamb, you will serve."

Walter Crane, "The Wolf and the Lamb" from *The Baby's Own Aesop*

Whichever word may apply, what matters is that "you / ewe will serve." The words, identically pronounced, put the distorter of words audibly in the right, from which he derives his right to satisfy his hunger. FRAUD AND VIOLENCE HAVE NO SCRUPLES—there are obviously certain "games that two can play at" in which one player can always count on winning.

Crane, for his part, helped to dress up *The Baby's Own Aesop* for socialists—or perhaps for cynics. His design of the page featuring wolf and lamb (which has already been discussed as showing the influence of Blake) is an obvious example. Here Crane combines two fables and establishes additional significance by spatial relationships between narrative elements. He confronts the lamb and the wolf with Aesop's hungry rooster, who has found jewelry instead of food. In this juxtaposition analogies on the falling diagonal attain rhetorical (or 'emphatic') significance. The string of pearls and the wolf showing his teeth have been moved into the center of the page. Here situated between the hungry rooster (IF HE ASK BREAD . . .) and the helpless victim of harassment, the lamb, they symbolize—as stone instead of bread (Matt. 7:9)[21] and as fraud and violence—the arrogance of wealth and power perpetually turned against the underprivileged—sheep and poultry. In "The Ass & the Sick Lion" (a plate I introduced a few pages back), the diagonal is again used for a significant confrontation. In that plate poet and artist, contrary to tradition, choose as the crafty lion's antagonist a donkey instead of a fox—certainly not by accident, for according to the apocryphal book *Jesus Sirach* (13:23), "the wild ass is the lion's prey in the desert: so also the poor are devoured by the rich."

Clearly Linton's verbal and Crane's visual signs show a new awareness of the political subtexts implied in fables which— apart from topical satire—had largely been interpreted as trans- porting the timeless wisdom of Aesop. In the guise of moral fables, traditional fable lore would teach the lessons that one always finds the wrong thing at the wrong time, that there is no way of arguing with wickedness, and that one had better think twice before taking risks. Crane's and Linton's art, of contrary impact, is that of political wolves in sheep's clothing.

As I have suggested earlier, theirs is an art of verbal and visual tropes and schemes, figures of transferred sense (metaphor and metonymy) and significant order. Eighteen out of the forty-eight plates in *The Baby's Own Aesop* present a similar collage of two fables on one page. This juxtaposition is particularly conducive to suggestive depicting as against mere illustrative or decorative picturing. Horizontal, vertical, or diagonal correlations between the images of agents and objects, interpreted by verbal echoes (or, as in the case of "the wild ass," by iconology and cultural heritage), create rich semiotic potential.

First a few notes on the transfer of sense. The additional meaning identified in the wolf/sheep/rooster/jewel plate on the basis of a chiastic arrangement of these four images is analogous to metonymy and metaphor. Clues to the readings of the sign vehicles are provided by the texts, but further "figures of speech and design" ensue. We see the jewel as a precious stone affixed to a chain of pearls, and we read of a "stone" useless to anybody "if he ask bread"—both suggest metonymically the stone that is thrown at beggars and metaphorically a heart of stone. A well- known metaphor for "fraud," "violence," and unscrupulousness (of which we read) is, of course, the wolf as we see him in the picture—while naming these features aims at people who are known to possess them, which is a metonymic substitution. Hence these metaphors and metonymies, both in word and im- age, pose the question of reference. Not that this would have been much of a problem at the time the book was published.

Since the 1850s, trade unionism had developed the new model of *amalgamated societies* (of engineers, spinners and weavers, builders and miners) providing for unemployment and dispute benefits. In the 1870s, there were frequent strikes for an in- crease in wages, sometimes following wage reductions that had been enforced by employers. Most of the strikes failed, however. The *sliding scales system* (under which wages were made to depend on the selling price of the product) had to be accepted in the coal fields due to the importation of blacklegs—as in 1874 in Lancashire, when the union leaders, on discouraging the blacklegs, were charged with conspiracy. In 1881, due to the depression of the later 1870s, unionism was largely crushed. In 1879 overall unemployment in Britain rose to nearly 12 percent, and 1885 and 1886 came to be the worst years of what is sometimes called a Great Depression. In 1887 when the *Aesop* came out, the first of a number of "new" unions began its fight against the contract system in the iron and steel trades. Under this system a small minority of skilled leading hands exploited the main body of workers by subemploying them at day wages while they themselves pocketed the money accruing under their much more favorable piecework contracts.

So much for "unscrupulousness" and "fraud." As for "violence," in 1886 a demonstration by the unemployed was shifted away from Trafalgar Square by the police. Stones were thrown into Pall Mall club windows. In this context, "Will ye give him a stone," quoted one year later, takes on an additional touch of sarcastic ambiguity, turning, as it does, a sign of humiliation into one of resistance. The year 1887—"a fatal year" (G. D. H. Cole)—saw the "Bloody Sunday" demonstrations when the government packed Trafalgar Square with soldiers and police, and demonstrators were injured.[22]

All the while Crane drew political cartoons and wrote prose fables of his own for Morris's *Commonweal* (1885–89) and other socialist papers. "The Vampire" from *Justice* (1885, printed in chapter 4) is representative of Crane's cartoons, in that metaphor ("the vampire Capitalism") and metonymy (a farm laborer as Labour) serve to create a plain, one-to-one allegory. However the epimythion (already quoted) to one of his own, non-Aesopian fables, in which a donkey casts off his "two masters," invites the reader to start off on his own and semioticize the tale much as I have just done with his *Aesop* plate:

> Comment or moral is, perhaps, superfluous; but if one should read "natural man" or "worker" for donkey, "land monopoly" for the first master, "capitalism" for the second, we can easily find details to fit "commercial competition," "the industrial system," and "the relation of labour to the employer," etc., in this homely fable.

"A Political Demonstration on the Way to Hyde Park" from *The Queen's London,*
1896

THE RHETORIC OF DEPICTION (III): SCHEMES AND THEIR REFERENCE

To discuss a domain of reference through figures of transferred meaning, I have started from an elementary scheme, a diagonal syntagm of images from two fables that suggests parallelism and contrast. There are, of course, more complex forms of significant ordering. Crane's collages in *The Baby's Own Aesop* offer much additional encouragement to "find details to fit" additional meaning.

I shall concentrate on a number of plates in which Crane, in fusing two fables, creates what I would like to call macrofables. Their content is in no way determined by the Aesopian corpus. Again through juxtaposition, contiguity or inclusion, similarity or contrast, images become available for semiotization, in accordance with texts on the page or in the readers' minds. More significantly the relations between the visual elements sometimes affect—and may even radically alter—the meanings of the limericks they accompany.

A rather trivial outcome of this rhetoric of confrontation is a loss of confidence in Aesop's time-honored ahistorical wisdom. For obviously the morals of two fables shown on one page can collide—which suggests that the Aesopian fable approximates a profound version of nonsense, giving, as it does, sauce to the goose as well as to the gander.[23] Thus a mouse and a lion in their miniepics simultaneously act out the power and the impotence of small fry in the presence of the high and mighty and the exchangeability of gender roles. One may "bite on iron" as the snake finds out—but, as the crafty fox knows, one may also get one's cheese in the end. It would seem that we don't get very far with that kind of insight when fraud and violence need pinning down.

The dominating strategy in Crane's macrofables is that of visual *paronomasia,* a play with similarities. Such similarities come across as highly suggestive, if often deceptive. Another close look at the macrofable just mentioned attests that obvious similarities foreground some of the signifiers—the raised head of the fox corresponding to that of the snake, the file corresponding to the tree, the tools to the branches, and the hardening fire to the "crow being weak." These correspondences signal, however, distinctions and contradictions between the signifieds. The images thus warn against facile identification, as the morals

:THE·MOUSE·&·THE·LION:

A POOR thing the Mouse
was, and yet,
When the Lion got
caught in a net,
All his strength was no use
'Twas the poor little Mouse
Who nibbled him out of the
net.

·SMALL·CAUSES·MAY·PRODUCE·GREAT·RESULT·

:THE·MARRIED·MOUSE:

SO the Mouse had Miss
Lion for bride;
Very great was his joy and
his pride:
But it chanced that she put
On her husband her foot,
And the weight was too much
So he died

·ONE·MAY·BE·TOO·AMBITIOUS·

Walter Crane, "The Mouse & the Lion" from *The Baby's Own Aesop*

do against the clichés of common sense: WE MAY MEET OUR
MATCH—*but then, flatterers may not.*

In juxtapositions of this sort, additional significance derives
from the convention that makes the reader interpret sequence
in space as sequence in time. Thus, two fable plots may, as it
were, be fused into a more comprehensive (and more significant) one. This can be shown in the plate combining "Horse and
Man" and "The Ass & the Enemy," which goes clearly beyond
a mere cautionary counterpointing of (possibly polysemous)
signifiers.

Both texts are already, in themselves, allegories containing

Walter Crane, "The Snake & the File" from *The Baby's Own Aesop*

social criticism. In yielding to a rider, the horse has sealed its fate as "slave" and "hack." The ass, goaded by its master into fleeing from "the Foe," can hardly hope for an improvement in its situation. Man is here accused of oppression and torment. Crane again underlines corresponding motifs by means of visual paronomasia, for example, the similar form and angle of the spear (above left) and the cudgel (below middle). (And again, similarities prove subtly, and provocatively, deceptive: Can hunting skills be equated with the exertion of brutal force?) In addition juxtaposition here creates a new "space of time" for both fables, extended and, as it were, cyclical, in which retribution

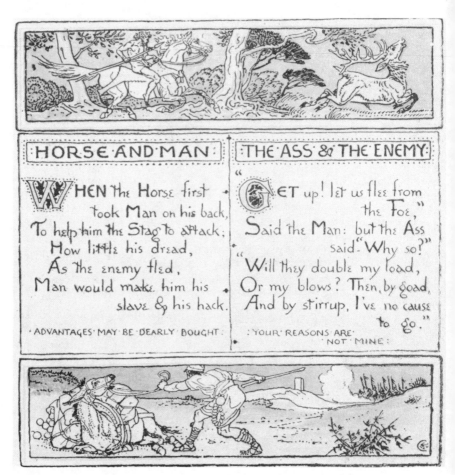

Walter Crane, "Horse and Man" from *The Baby's Own Aesop*

appears to have caught up with the oppressor or with oppression in general. Subverting the Aesopian common sense of ADVANTAGES MAY BE DEARLY BOUGHT, an optimistic macromoral of the new narrative might be "God brooks no goads." In fact the verbal paronomasia *God—goad* is exploited in Linton's text through the sarcastic pun "by goad." If, however, one pauses to consider "the Foe," on horseback, armed, and in full charge, a less optimistic macroplot would seem to reveal in the end a God of goads. In J. Hillis Miller's terms, Crane's subversion turns the tales of placid Aesop and preaching Linton into a composite text whose final message becomes undecidable.[24]

This device of depicting Aesop with "writerly" icons (to use one of Roland Barthes's terms)—a supply of signs for a text that the reader is induced to write himself—certainly seems to point to an attitude not so much of smiling detachment as of bitterness, if not cynicism. A final example will show how Crane's visual juxtapositions even tend to undermine Linton's texts as speech acts. The limericks, like the illustrations, become available for additional semiotization and show that they, too, have vestiges of marginal, weak coding hidden within them.

Opposite the plate we have just studied, we find a page on which Crane makes pictorial paronomasia explicit as the dominating structural device. Here the fables juxtaposed are "The Fox & the Mosquitoes" and "The Fox & the Lion." Four pictures are arranged symmetrically with the two interior pictures almost reflecting each other like mirror images. They represent the closing phase of the first and the opening phase of the second fable: the greater evil that one tries to avoid, the evil unknown that instills fear. Here, too, the sequence in space suggests interpretation as a sequence in time because both pictures evidently represent the same fox. As a result the Aesopian nursery moral of the second text (taken in isolation) is converted into its own sly caricature.

The first of the limericks (mentioned at the beginning of the previous section) has already gotten its political sting from its epimythion. Not only could everything be worse after all (the Aesopian reading), but THERE WERE POLITICIANS IN AESOP'S TIME, so let us keep those bloodsuckers who have at least stilled their hunger for the time being.

This is a story told from bitter experience. Now it is only in direct alignment with this insight that the second limerick reveals its submerged cynicism:

> The first time the Fox had a sight
> Of the lion, he 'most died of fright,
>   When he next met his eye
>   Fox felt just a bit shy:
> But the next quite at ease and polite.
> FAMILIARITY DESTROYS FEAR

This text represents two speech acts at the same time. It is plain and honest as a nursery instruction, but as such it is scornfully pooh-poohed and put up for derision as dangerously naive. "Have no fear of strangers," says the pedagogical voice. "You

Walter Crane, "The Fox & the Mosquitoes" from *The Baby's Own Aesop*

should never, little fox," answers the skeptic within the same words, "forget your fear, whether of mosquitoes or lions."

Tzvetan Todorov and Wlad Godzich, translating the Russian semiotician Mikhail Bakhtin, have called this device hybrid speech and subsumed it under the more general term interior dialogue. The words show no signals of irony, yet their context reveals in them a gap between two intentionalities.[25] Only as part of a macrotext, of word and image linked together, do the verses remind the reader that good sense, fear, and caution often get lost through force of habit and that resignation, however wise under certain circumstances, is more often mere tail-wagging contentment, uncritical ease, and servility.

To Summarize and End with Gentleness

Crane's *The Baby's Own Aesop* is an illustrated book that not only pictures Aesop's tales but teases the reader's imagination by various depiction devices or "pointing." Its illustrations play off two visual codes against each other—a strong one that represents mimetically the agents and plots of Aesop's tales, and a weaker one that, by means of horizontal and vertical repetition and framing, segmentation and combination, identification, similarity and difference creates semiotic potential. In what might be seen as a dissemination of meaning, the text suggests and simultaneously limits visual signifieds, while visual correlations, in their turn, resemioticize the text.

Roland Posner, in his general semiotics of culture, speaks of a reciprocal flexibilization of paralyzed codes and regards such interactions of codes as a recurrent and vital part of cultural processes. It is tempting to expand on Posner's metaphor, using an image favored by Hillis Miller: we see children (including those who regard themselves as adults) learning in a playful way from Crane's *Aesop* that one can act wisely by stepping aside

CARICATURE OF A PAGE OF *BABY'S OWN ÆSOP*
By Mrs. Houghton

Ellen Houghton, "With Apologies to *Baby's Aesop*"

at the right moment when Wisdom and Experience raise their fingers—in a lateral dance into imagination. The world looks different from that angle.[26]

Incidentally the plate showing the fox and the lion was made the subject of a little parody—the signifiers entering into a lateral dance of their own. One day, after a visit to the Cranes, Ellen Houghton, a cousin of Walter Crane's and an illustrator in her own right, took up her pen for a humorous homage to the artist.[27] Aesop and Edward Lear, Linton and Walter Crane were all put into the harness of an anecdote. The king of the animals, Walter Crane's ambiguously innocent monster with folded paws, is called upon to pay a compliment. The artist with his mop of fuzzy hair overcomes the shyness of a lap-dog with smiles and friendliness as we observe how

GENTLENESS CONQUERS JILL.

8

"Let Beasts Bear Gentle Minds"—Fable into Animal Biography

"Since men prove beasts, let beasts bear gentle minds."
—William Shakespeare, *The Rape of Lucrece*

"REALITY" AS DISCOURSE

WHEN, in 1862, the young Walter Crane finished his five-year apprenticeship as a designer and engraver in Linton's shop, he earned his first money with illustrations that were very different from *The Baby's Own Aesop*. He designed wood engravings for children's books with tales from everyday life. In 1869, for example, he did eight full-page plates for *The Magic of Kindness* by the brothers Mayhew, and in 1877 it was seven plates for "Ennis Graham's" *The Cuckoo Clock*. Later for many years he illustrated books by Agnes de Havilland, who, under her maiden name "Mrs. Molesworth," produced a never-ending line of so-called *children's romances*.

In the last quarter of the nineteenth century, romances that were specifically written for children flooded the book market. Disraeli's Act of 1876 had instituted compulsory education for roughly 3 million children and thereby created a vast readership that was clamorous for new books. This was, as Percy Muir puts it, the "period of the rattling good yarn"—vide Robert Louis Stevenson, Henry Rider Haggard, or Anthony Hope. But although these authors and others who followed in their wake are still being read nowadays and their tales of adventure, exotic or Ruritanian, continue to be exploited by the media, the more modest variant of the romance for younger children is forgotten—hardly more than occasional quaint items in secondhand book shops.

Here adventures were presented as looming just outside the

children's homes or, at the most, a day's trip away. At least this was what Agnes de Havilland, "Mrs. Molesworth," set out to show. Of her domestic romances published between 1875 and 1890, those which Crane illustrated had titles like *Tell Me a Story, Grandmother Dear, The Tapestry Room: A Child's Romance, The Adventure of Herr Baby, Rosy, Us, Christmas Tree Land, Four Winds Farm, Little Miss Peggy: Only a Nursery Story, A Christmas Child: A Sketch of a Boy's Life, The Rectory Children,* or *The Children of the Castle.* In 1888 (up to which year Allibone lists thirty-four Molesworth titles), a critic wrote that "Mrs. Molesworth . . . is the best story-teller for children England has yet known,"[1] and others agreed. But by then the market for children's books had become fiercely competitive, books were commissioned, and even Mrs. Molesworth's gentle and domestic world was invaded by at least two dozen other women writers, "with a great family likeness between their productions."[2]

Large editions proved the success of the formula suggested by the titles I have quoted. These nursery stories or children's romances presented "sketches" of children's lives and little adventures in the city and the country. They are readable, informative, and gently educational novelettes without the goody-goody moralizing of the stories that could be found in temperance and religious magazines, let alone the heavy educational barrage of Thomas Day's dreary *Sandford and Merton* (1783–89), which had been prominent among the small number of children's books up to the middle of the century. They prodded their little readers toward right thinking and good behavior by means of concrete examples in narrative and dialogue, which gave them a systematic training in right and good *speaking.* In other words, the child's world and behavior were categorized and given orthodox codings as positive and negative, with gradations between prescribed and forbidden. The resulting networks of signifiers were ordered around *final vocabularies* (a concept recently proposed by Richard Rorty),[3] the central terms of value to which people refer when they judge things as normal, natural, moral, culturally valuable, or perhaps just commonsensical. "Good" and "bad," "nice" and "not nice," and "gentle" and "rude" constituted the favored centers of these vocabularies, and their frequent repetition cut up daily life into clearly defined routines.

Only rarely did these narratives show marks of tension under their rough-hewn semantics and pragmatics. With the excuse of giving merely an elementary grounding, they had no truck with ambiguities and internal contradictions, the dependence of all

"Are— are you a mermaid, or a that other thing?' asked the child." p. 156

Walter Crane, "Are—are you a mermaid?" from Mary Louisa Molesworth, *The Children of the Castle*

linguistic signs on their interpretants,[4] and the necessity of interpreting these interpretants in their turn. In what follows I will analyze one such text and discuss some of the problems that may have arisen from its use of variants of discourse and their possible conflicts.[5] The point I want to make is that oscillations and topical multiplications of meaning similar to those observed in Lytton's fables and Crane's illustrations were bound to occur in apparently simple and straightforward texts like these as well—due to discursive conflicts muted by only a very flimsy effect of what might be termed (with regard to the word's etymology) "unison." The text will be taken from a subclass of domestic children's romances which blended realism with fantasy. These books, extended narratives in which animals think, speak, act, and gather experiences like humans, may be called (after a title of 1820) *animal biographies.*[6] But "like" poses a problem: man and beast may well be divided rather than connected by their ability to speak.

In 1877 Anna Sewell (1820–78) published her only book, *Black Beauty: The Autobiography of a Horse.*[7] It is the fictitious autobiography of a gelding, the account of his carefree childhood in the country, a short time of happiness and good work pulling carriages, then maltreatment, an accident, hard labor as a cab horse in London, until, finally, by a merciful act of providence, he ends up in the hands of kind owners again. In a way this is (in Moleswortheese) *Tell Me a Story of The Magic of Kindness in Four Winds Farm, A Sketch of a Horse's Life: A Child's Romance,* and, as will be shown in a moment, even *Grandmother Dear* is not far away. In the last decades under Queen Victoria, Anna Sewell's book could be found in almost any nursery of the bourgeoisie.

Its immediate success "brought forth a crop of similar works employing every type of animal, reptile, insect, and even plants (Quayle)."[8] But of these *Black Beauty* alone was to become a classic of English children's literature, and it has been in print ever since. It is just possible that this is due not to an overly seductive simplicity but, quite on the contrary, to a floating of meaning that the text suggests on various levels. As in *Gulliver's Travels* one and a half centuries earlier, *Black Beauty's* discursive ambivalence is situated within a worldview—as projected by its fable-related plot, its characters, and its explicit thematic statements—that is far less unified (or, in Stevenson's words, capable of being "resumed in any succinct formula") than its reputation as an edifying childrens' book might suggest.

First Formation of Discourses—Fantasy (The Imaginary) versus Exhortation

As in fables, in *Black Beauty* the animals are able to communicate with each other, though not with men. They do so in a way that would have appeared perfectly familiar to a Victorian child. On the very first page, the foal hears its mother (and the listening child its mother) giving advice in a voice that indicates, and sets great store by, good upbringing:

> "I wish you to pay attention to what I am going to say to you. The colts who live here are very good colts, but they are cart-horse colts, and of course they have not learned manners. You have been well-bred and well-born; your father has a great name in these parts, and your grandfather won the cup two years at the Newmarket races; your grandmother had the sweetest temper of any horse I ever knew, and I think you have never seen me kick or bite. I hope you will grow up gentle and good, and never learn bad ways; do your work with a good will, lift your feet up well when you trot, and never bite or kick even in play."[9]

And Black Beauty recapitulates:

> I have never forgotten my mother's advice; I knew she was a wise old horse, and our master thought a great deal of her.

A wise old horse, indeed. These words, a stock phrase used here with additional, and surprisingly literal, meaning, invite a smile. A great deal of the text is developed along this pattern of restoring an unfamiliar literalness to familiar sayings. Everyday English (like other languages) is full of equine metaphors. The text gives them a good trot out. On the other hand, the language of horse husbandry gives additional meanings to the most familiar expressions. "I never knew that horses picked up stones before," a driver has to admit. They do, as we learn when Black Beauty gets a loose scattered piece of flint very tightly wedged into one of his forefeet, which is called "picking up a stone."

This semantic filling up of familiar speech by means of reliteralization and a specialized register makes the worlds of horse and man, as it were, mutually transparent. "We trotted up nearer to see what went on. 'Bad boy!' he said, 'bad boy!'"—a frightened glance from human eyes over one's hooves. "It makes them vicious . . . they are like children, train 'em up in the way they should go, as the good book says, and when they are old they will not depart from it." Here moral wisdom seems to be derived from the horse trainer's manual. It may be assumed that this linguistic dressage has a twofold effect: it weakens narrative reference—do we see, in "we trotted up," a foal or a human child jogging along?—while increasing the text's semiotic potential. I will try to give a more detailed account of the way these effects make the text oscillate between fantasy and exhortation.

Technically speaking, most of the text's passages can be allocated to one of two speech acts—or, occasionally, to both. For one thing, Black Beauty's narrative is full of signals that entice the young reader or listener into an almost physical sharing of experiences. Identification constantly is invited and, as in Lacan's theory of the Imaginary,[10] pursued up to the point where it clashes with reality, and the shock of mis-recognition produces an increase of imaginative desire. "Let us cheer up and have a run to the other end of the orchard," Merrylegs suggests to his friend Black Beauty six lines from the end of a chapter (which might prompt the person reading to the child to make exactly the same suggestion), "(so we) got up our spirits by munching some very sweet apples" (a possible follow-up for the child) "which lay scattered on the grass." End of chapter, a break in the reading, a return to matters at hand. At moments like these, Anna Sewell shows great skill in handling her oscillating signifiers so as to create fantasy as a mirror phenomenon of reality, tantalizing in its cheerful deceit.

At the same time, her blending of the experiental domains of horse and child contributes significantly to the formation of signs which, according to Lacan, belong to the Symbolic, the semiotic space in which one is assigned one's position(s) as a social subject, that is, to the text's impact as exhortation. This impact is in itself of two kinds: admonishment and "influence."

SUBFORMATION OF DISCOURSES (EXHORTATION)— (A) ADMONISHMENT (THE SYMBOLIC)

For one thing, the book admonishes children (and adults) to treat animals better—*Black Beauty* has been rightly praised for its strictures against the bearing rein, the gag bit, blinkers, and docked tails. At times Sewell's pleading has a rather sinister aspect, though. Thrown into the bargain are atrocious images of "little puppies . . . (having) . . . the soft flap of their pretty little ears cut quite off . . . Why don't they cut their own children's ears into points?" Significantly this oedipal scenario is marked by unnecessary expansion: "Why don't they cut the end off their (children's) noses to make them look plucky?" While this is the harangue of a stallion, Black Beauty feels the same revulsion ("I found a bitter feeling towards men rise up in my mind"), and Ginger, a chestnut mare, reacts "much excited . . . declaring that men were both brutes and blockheads." Ginger has already suffered from sharp bits that "hurt my tongue and jaw, and the blood from my tongue coloured the froth that kept flying from my lips." Consequently, "I had made up my mind that men were my natural enemies and that I must defend myself."

It is difficult not to read "men" in these outcries as gendered, and to hear in them a hateful denunciation of what Lacan calls the phallus as the signifier of "cultural privileges and positive values which define male subjectivity within patriarchal society" (Kaja Silverman). The book may even be read (as Ruth Padel puts it) "almost as one of the great feminist texts," regardless of Black Beauty's sex—and he is male, notwithstanding Margaret Drabble's original summary in *The Oxford Companion to English Literature* ("the life of a black mare").[11] It is quite consistent that among the book's dramatic personae the human females (with the exception of one "tall, proud-looking" aristocrat) should be "nice," "sweet," and "gentle," about which more will be said in a moment.

As a projection of sexual anxiety, the fear of torture and death dealt out by men lurks but thinly disguised under Anna Sewell's humane pleading. In all this her reliteralizations are of considerable help to her. Thus the horses' pleasure in being able to "hold their heads up" (and not have them "held up" by the bearing-rein, at the time a fashionable, though painful tool) is not only given a refreshed literal meaning but becomes one of the book's central images of a protest against degradation through violence and the infliction of pain ("those horrid bits that I was tortured with in London"). Conversely "going to the dogs" has a ghastly ring to it when Black Beauty comes close to being sold, by his brutal owner named Skinner (whose "mouth was as full of teeth as a bulldog's"), to the knacker, for dogs' meat and his skin: "Then he must go to the dogs." The gelding escapes "skinning" (be it metaphorically or in dire fact) in the nick of time, when he is bought by a grandfather, whose pleasure it is "to make old horses young," at the pleading of his little grandson. Black Beauty recovers, begins really "to feel quite young again," and is finally sold to three sisters who treat him kindly and put him out to grass, "so I have nothing to fear." These fantasies can easily be read as manifestations of the Freudian family romance, with a powerful exorcism of the father.

The signifiers of the Imaginary and the Symbolic, if subjected to interpretative processes, enter into various networks with transindividual versions of Reality. A recent model of psycho-analytical semiotics, which covers these networks to a greater extent than the Lacanians do, has been proposed by Antony Easthope in his book *Poetry and Phantasy* (1989).[12] Easthope claims that imaginative literature "offers a phantasy [*sic*] to a subject." That is, it offers a wish fulfillment through fiction in scenic or narrative form, which may be analyzed according to the Freudian matrix—but it is a phantasy that is *public,* not *private.* As such literature has unconscious effects as well as conscious content. Because its aesthetic is not an essence but a function operating between the text and its reader, the text as a verbal construct is transversed by social and historical as well as private meanings. Pleasure in the signifiers (the words) facilitates pleasure in the social phantasy. These assumptions may help to put Anna Sewell's discursive oscillations between the Imaginary and the Symbolic within a frame of reality in the sense of nineteenth-century reception aesthetics.

SUBFORMATION OF DISCOURSES (EXHORTATION)— (B) "INFLUENCE" (THE REAL)

Victorian prescriptive literature on child-rearing shows that there was growing concern in middle-class families about the diminishing effectiveness of the religious and social authorities, as well as fear of the corrosive effects of egalitarian values on parental authority in particular. By 1843 as one tract puts it, "the great principles of liberty and equal rights . . . have penetrated even into the quiet havens of domestic life." Consequently the importance attached to the family as society's chief formative agency was greatly stepped up. John Locke's idea that children were almost infinitely malleable, plastic creatures merged with a diminishing belief in original sin and child depravity. The Scottish moral philosophers (Hutcheson, Reid) contributed their assumptions on "character formation" based on a training of the moral faculties by means of "influence." Stephen Mintz has collected rich material from contemporary advice literature to show that influence was one of the period's central concerns in education: a number of "silent and imperceptible" methods to foster sensitivity to social conventions and rules.[13]

Female influence, in particular, was seen as effective in replacing both physical coercion and the psychological pressure of earlier "tales of abandonment, castration, and divine punishment" (Mintz). What counted was the subtler method of appealing "invisibly" to the young people's incipient sense of right and wrong. Mothers were called on to graft discipline in their children by furnishing them with examples of "kindness and cheerfulness" (Lydia M. Child, 1831) or "the most absolute confidence, and an unchecked good will" (Isaac Taylor, 1838). Although obedience remained a primary goal, it had to be "cheerful," free, and voluntary, and instilled through loving submission to the mother's expectations and an instinctive desire for affection. Discussions of female influence emphasized that the cultivation of character traits traditionally viewed as symbols of inferiority—self-restraint, self-denial, sacrifice, suppressing one's aggressive impulses—was of central importance. The aim was no longer to enforce moral prohibitions and rigid behavioral standards but to internalize good manners by appealing to the child's love: "There is no constraint like that of love," Heman Humphrey wrote in 1840.

In short—robust authority was out, loving kindness was in. Books, studied in seclusion or read out by mother, were counted among the most effective means to further these pedagogical aims. *Black Beauty* evidently fits these coordinates. "I wish you to pay attention" (the beginning of the first quotation and one of Sewell's many polysemous passages) identifies the speech act as one of persuasion, be it in an open field or speaking to one's child in a Victorian *bel étage*. "I hope you will grow up gentle and good, and never learn bad ways; do your work with a good will"—an emotional appeal to the child's (or colt's) voluntary and loving assent. Then a glance aside: "They are cart-horse colts and of course they have not learned manners"—education through a subtle insinuation of correct speech which implies a social "fact" that goes without saying. As for self-restraint, at one point Black Beauty proudly says: "I could have groaned, for I was suffering intense pain ... but horses are used to bearing their pain in silence. I uttered no sound." Ginger, his companion, when overstrained, has "too much spirit to complain." As for self-government, the old horse's teaching is clearly an appeal to internalize examples held up to him: "Your grandmother had the sweetest temper ... you have never seen *me* kick or bite."

It is characteristic of this fictitious context of female "influence" that all we are told about Black Beauty's father is that he "has a great name in these parts," whereas his mother sets the tone of gentleness and sweetness that pervades the book down to the three sisters, "my ladies," of the last paragraph.

SECOND FORMATION OF DISCOURSES—TRADITIONAL MORALS VERSUS PRAGMATICS

So far the oscillation in Anna Sewell's *Black Beauty* of numerous speech segments between human speech and animal speech has been discussed sporadically in the (ahistorical) Lacanian scenarios of the Imaginary and the Symbolic. I have further suggested that these findings can be related to sociohistorical reality in the light of Easthope's hypothesis that imaginative literature offers a public phantasy in the process of subject formation and interpreted them as tributary to a subtle technique of influence in Victorian child-rearing. However Sewell's language game may be seen as an even more direct (because purely intralinguistic) reflection of the Real in the Foucaldian sense: that which is accorded consent and authority in the contemporary set of conflicting discourse formations.[14] I want to focus on an example of discursive conflict in Victorian England that was conspicuous enough for some of Anna Sewell's contemporaries. To make this clear, the intriguing double edge of the book's language will now have to be given a closer scrutiny, which means returning to Rorty's concept of final vocabularies as introduced at the beginning of this chapter.

In a manner of speaking, *Black Beauty* trots from pun to pun. Cases of irony show that Sewell was conscious of subtly introducing her young readers or listeners to figurative language: "This was the first experience I had of men's kindness, it was all force." Likewise her reliteralizations help to create a pleasurable competence in metaphor. "Lift your feet well when you trot," an admonishment possibly heard and hated many times, is set in a new context that leads through fancy to impersonation and delight. It is naughty to "kick or bite"—these words, addressed to a colt, make new sense to the child. "To breed," "gentle," "good," "bad ways," or "work" fit into this humorous double entendre that may well have served to provide a linguistic training as well as the obvious pedagogical one.

But apart from furthering rhetorical competence, the text

may owe part of its continued success to a more radical fissure in many of its signifiers. There is good reason to speak of a plot of discourses in *Black Beauty,* which introduces the child to a set of pragmatic speech phenomena which occur frequently in everyday communication—the use of ambivalent signs that belong (often undecidably) to conflicting vocabularies implying quite different value systems. *Black Beauty* displays the clash of two such networks or vocabularies. This is where, in spite of the rather relaxed trot of its episodic plot structure, Sewell's tale turns into a veritable tournament: in *Black Beauty* man and beast are divided rather than connected by their ability to speak.

In horse language (as the quotations have indicated), experience and insight revolve around a small number of traditional values and moral attitudes:

The colts that live here are very good colts.

I hope you will grow up gentle and good, and never learn bad ways; do your work with a good will.

Ginger did her work honestly, and did her full share . . . Rory, the horse that mostly went with me . . . a good, honest fellow he was.

Our master was a good, kind man. . . . We were all fond of him, and my mother loved him very much.

"There are good masters and good grooms beside ours, though of course ours are the best." This wise speech of good little Merrylegs . . . was quite true.

Utterances of this kind are index signs beyond their conventional communicative sign content: they characterize their speakers as being themselves "good," "gentle," "kind," "honest," and inclined to be "loving." Throughout the book events and experiences involving the horses are identified and interpreted by means of plain words like these, within a code of perception and evaluation that is not differentiated any further. Thus to take but one of these signifiers, a new coachman, in Black Beauty's view, is "so gentle and kind," another "just as gentle and pleasant," there is "no gentleness" in a third, a fourth is "gentle and very clever," and a little girl who tries to keep his load light, is "my gentle friend."

"Gentleness" relates to the nineteenth-century context of the female civilizing influence mentioned before, but a more traditional model of this rough-hewn vocabulary is obvious. The old horse's admonishment not to "learn bad ways" but to do one's "work with a good will" points, of course, to the "good will" of the Scriptures and the "man of good will" in the *Book of Common Prayer,* both as yet unrivaled for formative patterns of speech.[15] The polarity of "good will" and "learn bad ways" was worked out emphatically in Apprentice Guides and similar educational tracts, which from the eighteenth century onward contrasted honest work with sloth and vice; one has but to think of "The Two Shoemakers" in Hannah More's *Cheap Repository Tracts* (1795–98). Of course Hogarth's *Industry and Idleness Exemplified, in the Conduct of Two Fellow 'Prentices* (1747) comes to mind, with the artist's own commentary: "The one (Goodchild) taking good courses . . . becomes a valuable man."[16] To return for a moment to a point I made in my synopsis of prose fables in chapter 4, the castigation of idleness had been a prominent feature of eighteenth-century children's books as well, vide Isaac Watts,

> In Works of Labour or of Skill
>   I would be busy too:
> For Satan finds some Mischief still
>   For idle hands to do.[17]

From the beginning of the nineteenth century onward, this was projected into the animal and insect world as, for example, in "Velvet and Busy; or, Idleness and Industry": "Velvet, though she was so pretty, she was not good . . . Busy, who was only a plain brown bee, was at work from morning till night."[18] *Black Beauty* thus falls into line with a general set of precepts: be loving and good, do your work willingly, avoid bad habits and vice, and you will in time become (whether as bee or horse, woman or man) the epitome of Victorian Christian righteousness.

However, in Anna Sewell's days, these beautiful linguistic coins already had another side to them, which indicated their cash value. In *Black Beauty* the horses are confronted with humans (characteristically they are all males) in whose discourse the words "good," "gentle," "sweet-tempered," "spirit," "bad habits," "vice," and even "character" oscillate between an everyday and a technical meaning. The principle is easy to see: a "good horse," in human language, is obviously a far cry from what being "good" in (imaginary) horse language entails. True, when speaking un-technically, men use these value words very much like the horses—"be good and kind to man and beast" is a coachman's favorite maxim. But their technical language is concerned, first and foremost, with something very different—utility.

Talking about the handling of horses implies a reshuffling of the signifiers mentioned so far around the central signifier effectiveness. "Drive him gentle," as an order to a coachman, indicates a way to use the reins. As descriptions of the horses, the positive terms mean (to men) no more than tractability, which in equine language has its own sarcastic translation: to be (in the words of Ginger, the chestnut mare) "a quiet, humble, obedient piece of horse-flesh." When Ginger is rather restless and irritable, a coachman says that "she'll be as good as Black Beauty by and by." And, indeed, "gentle" she becomes. "Is he gentle?" a child asks about Black Beauty—"gentle as your own kitten," is the answer. "Gentle" here equals "quiet" ("quiet and pleasant as he could be," "a pleasanter creature I never wished to mount"). Even "sweet" indicates no more than docility: "a sweet good-tempered face." A horse's good "character" is its fitness to do its job. "Spirit," it is true, may mean a horse's temperament but is often wrongly ascribed to what is the result of men's cruelty for the sake of "fashion." Thus a proud bearing and a foaming mouth, when taken for "spirit," may be, in fact, signs of discomfort and strain under the bearing rein: "'What fine, spirited creatures!' . . . I felt worn and depressed." As for the "bad habits" Black Beauty was admonished to shun, "a slovenly way of driving gets a horse into bad habits"—for example, a lack of grace and efficacy. Of course the word "vice" itself, in horsebreeding, denotes mere unruliness. "Good" horses are "free from vice," bad handling "makes them vicious."

The clash of the two discourses over one word is particularly violent in the contrast between the horse mother's initial admonition to "do your work with good will" and Skinner's "my plan is to work 'em as long as they'll go, and then sell 'em for what they'll fetch." The suggestion seems to be that humans, by having developed registers of utility that the speech of animals lacks, have made a decisive step away from innocence. This step means acquiring power over others. Power, according to Michel Foucault, is not exclusively a matter of institutions and social positions, but an ongoing process that is largely a linguistic one.[19] The multiplication of networks within which signifiers function is one way (often difficult to see through) of manipulating and disciplining others. As in "gentle," "good," and "spirit," "work them" may claim approval due to a moral coding ("give them work to do"), when, in fact, mere utility ("make them operate") is at stake.

In the final part of *Black Beauty,* economic interest is shown to prevail cruelly over what had initially been presented, in horse speech, as beautiful ideas. The same words are now used as distorting mirrors to evoke reflection and sympathy in the reader. Under harsh competition, when large cab-owners like Skinner let out horses to drivers for a fixed sum a day and the latter have to "work" fourteen to sixteen hours per day (Sundays included) to support their large families, "'tis a mockery to tell a man that he must not overwork his horse." Thus in the ironies of one word, morality questions exploitation ("to 'work' 'em as long as they'll go"), while economic considerations question morality ("a mockery to tell a man [not to] 'overwork' his horse"). This goes far beyond Anna Sewell's playful polysemies which blend the worlds of the child and the colt. As I will try to show now, it can be seen as a symptom of a general uneasiness of the Victorians about semantic oscillations in value words, a slippage within a systematic social formation of discourses. The speeches in Anna Sewell's *Black Beauty* partake in what has been recently called an *interdiscourse.*[20]

In this view the horses' plain words, their technical reinterpretations, and their practical perversions reflect the debate on utilitarianism in the decades before *Black Beauty* was published. Here as in the case of a "good" horse, "the ultimate good" was hotly contested—usefulness and the power to please, to be conducive to general happiness, stood against what Raymond Williams, following Arnold, has called "the traditional idea of man's business as 'the pursuit of perfection.'"[21] Early in the century, Coleridge had condemned the "accursed practice of ever considering only what seems expedient for the occasion ... of never listening to the true and unerring impulses of our better nature." In this line of thought, John Stuart Mill's book *Utilitarianism* (1861) was an attempt to reinvest "pleasure" and "happiness" with some of their more traditional values by freeing these words from their terminological linkage with "circumstantial advantages" like security, permanence, economy, and effectiveness.[22]

Matthew Arnold, in *Culture and Anarchy* (1869), pitted the idea of "the study of perfection" against the "pursuit of the production of wealth, not an absolute good in itself."[23] Similarly John Ruskin, from *Unto This Last* (1860) onward, had made harsh pronouncements against the fashionable displacing of central terms like "wealth" from their original moral context into a pragmatic one. For Ruskin, "wealth," "the possession of articles of value," could only be "what was good for life," what had "value ... the life-giving power of anything" (*Munera Pulveris,* 1872). One year before *Black Beauty* appeared, Ruskin reminded his readers in one of his open letters called *Fors Clavigera* (1876) that one talked about "a man's 'Goods,' not a man's 'Bads'"—meaning "the good things which he has honestly got and can skilfully use."[24] Ginger, believing that "bad words were made for bad things" (and thus, good words for good), would have whinnied assent.

About 1880, realist novels occasionally echoed the debate. In Henry James' *Washington Square* (1881) the pious question "Do you think it is better to be clever than to be good?" meets with the answer, "Good *for what?* . . . You are good for nothing unless you are clever." This systematic conflict of discourses had long since produced utopian fictions (Coleridge's *clerisy,* Carlyle's *heroes*), among which *Black Beauty* may be placed as a modest contribution. Matthew Arnold's vision, for instance, in *Culture and Anarchy*—eight years before *Black Beauty* was published—is well known. Let a number of "aliens," he suggested, human beings led "by a general humane spirit," "with a bent . . . for simply concerning themselves with reason and the will of God," work to awaken the "best self" that is latent in all men but is obscured by class ideology and habit. Emerging in all classes, "they have, in general, a rough time of it in their lives." In their efforts poetry will set a standard of "beauty, and of a human nature perfect on all sides."[25] If, with the plot's unfolding, Black Beauty, honest, gentle, and long-suffering, may have suggested to some of its readers an incarnation of moral beauty as well (thus reverting the direction of the pragmatic transfer of signifiers), contemporary cultural criticism was clearly an important context.

FABLE COMPONENTS IN THE BOOK'S REALISM

The preceding analysis of *Black Beauty* has focused on a number of discourses that are systematically related to one another. Like the visual structures in Walter Crane's *Aesop,* this discourse formation within one book has suggested a link-up with other topical discourses, a resemiotization that adds to the meanings of plot, character, and theme. However the resulting signifiers in the domains of the Imaginary, the Symbolic, and the Real can be easily reconnected with the more obvious sign content of the narrative agents, actions, and isotopies.

One obvious relationship is that of intensifying an awareness of plot-inherent problems. If being "good" as a horse means being useful through docility, endurance, and self-restraint—does this also apply when its rider is "madly drunk"? When he cuts into the horse with his whip to make it gallop at top speed while one of its hooves is split down to the very quick? When the end is foreseeably the horse's ruin for life and the man's death?

This problem, which underlies the plot of chapter 25 of *Black Beauty,* leads us back to the issue of unitary parabolic meaning. Since we have placed Anna Sewell's book in the nineteenth-century debate on invisible "influence" in child-rearing, this is the place to add that Steven Mintz, in surveying his material, does not hesitate to speak of a "psychological *manipulation*" to attain, by means of internalized discipline and self-denial, only a more effectual and lasting form of filial obedience, "the foundation of principles of duty and order that would carry over into public life."[26] Although this is a retrospective view, even in those days chapter 25 would seem to have prompted questions not easy to answer. At the plot's climax, the incident of the mad driver plays off "good will" and submission against something that is, in Derrida's term, the book's supplement—not in it, yet at every moment presupposed by it and ready to take over—resistance and rebellion.[27] But an unwritten complement it remains: "Men are strongest," Ginger, the chestnut mare, sighs, "and if they are cruel and have no feeling, there is nothing that we can do, but just bear it, bear it on and on to the end."

Clearly a plot that involves domestic horses, so clearly dependent on man, has no place for rebellion, or even a considered form of refusal and disobedience. No mestangs grazed on England's plains as they did in the United States described by Aesop Junior in 1834.[28] Just as clearly the discourse components discussed as related to the Imaginary (sensuous pleasure), the Symbolic (fear of castration), and the Real (good will versus exploitation) point to revolt. It is hardly surprising that this unresolved conflict should be mirrored where *Black Beauty* incorporates, as narrative substructures, variants of the contemporary parabolic fable.[29] Far from being unified, the book's numerous insets of parabolic material veer between desperate incrimination and smug acceptance.

Several chapters of the book are modeled on the pattern set by the numerous fables "for the nursery" which flooded the market after 1800 and have been discussed at an earlier point. Like Anne Jane Cupples's *Fables Illustrated by Stories from Real Life* (1874, three years before *Black Beauty*), these chapters moralize events that children would have witnessed themselves, ending pat with a memorable dictum. Thus in line with many religious and temperance fables,[30] Sewell tells a tale about another drunken driver whose recklessness ruins a horse for life; she has a cabman cry out: "If there's one devil that I should like to see in the bottomless pit more than another, it's the drink devil." Chapter 39 tells of the cabman who had called it "a mockery to tell a man that he must not overwork his horse" dying from overwork himself, and ends: "No one spoke for a while, and then the Governor said, 'I tell you what, mates, this is a warning for us.'" Chapter 40 ends with Black Beauty pondering a particularly revolting scene: "Oh! if men were more merciful, they would shoot us before we came to such misery." These are clearly parable epimythia and, as such, outcries against the state of things.

However, at other times, closer to Cupples's *Fables Illustrated by Stories,* Sewell uses short set pieces which, in their pious confidence, have a comforting rather than an irritating effect. Thus what has before been presented through horse-language as pure torture, is rather played down when "a lady (with) a sweet earnest voice" delivers a sermon against the bearing rein, shows the carter that Black Beauty can draw a heavier load without it, and steps aside again pronouncing the episode's "application": "I thank you for trying my plan with your good horse, and I am sure you will find it far better than the whip." Quite at the other end of the scale, a chapter headed "The Sunday Cab" is an edifying parable of a cabman who, resisting strong temptation, does not give up his Sundays and nevertheless retains the patronage of his favorite customer. This chapter ends: "If a thing is right, it can be done, and if it is wrong, it can be done without." Thus parabolic insets, attaching themselves to the book's discursive conflicts (pragmatics versus ethics, unitary meaning versus ambiguity and duplicity), import into it a broad spectrum of attitudes between righteous indignation and smugness.

If the plot as a whole has a parabolic meaning, it is at least as double-edged as the book's presentation of human discourse, its muted theme of resistance, and its assemblage of parabolic insets. True, to summarize what has been presented on various levels of meaning, life's misery, an incessant suffering, and human cruelty appear to be recurrent issues. The main plot of suffering is given a parallel subplot. Whereas the gelding is disfigured from his fall under the drunkard, Ginger, the chestnut mare, gets ruined by hard riding. "And so here we are," the mare considers halfway through the book, "ruined in the prime of our youth and strength, you by a drunkard, and I by a fool." Then the gelding is sold as a job horse and later has to serve as a cab horse in London. After Ginger has gone downhill in a similar way, the companions meet once more. "Men are strongest . . . they are cruel and have no feeling, there is nothing that we can do." This depressive résumé, already quoted, occurs towards the end of the book. A little later a dead chestnut horse is carried past, its "lifeless tongue slowly dropping [sic] with blood."

Yet this lurid scenario will be replaced in its turn. In the remaining section of the book, several figures, most of them females, show deep concern for Black Beauty. There is his "gentle friend," the girl who tries to get him relieved of his heavy load ("I am sure it is very cruel") and the lady who pleads against using the bearing rein. When one Mr. Thoroughgood, to please his little grandson, saves Black Beauty from the knacker and three ladies buy him for easy work and leisure, the author has succumbed to "sweetness" and "gentleness" one more time and muted her earlier project. And here, too, intertextuality provides the tools.

With a glimmer of hope, Black Beauty is permitted to take leave of his listeners:

> My ladies have promised that I shall never be sold, and so I have nothing to fear; and here my story ends.

To present-day readers, this has an unmistakably Victorian ring. Take *David Copperfield*:

> And now my written story ends. I look back, once more . . . I see myself, with Agnes at my side, journeying along the road of life.
>
> O Agnes, O my soul, so may thy face be by me when I close my life indeed.

Of course "readers of the time were especially loud in begging for cheerfully reassuring endings" (M. M. Kenda).[31] The parallelism reminds us that Black Beauty's tale is, as David Copperfield puts it, a "written story," too. Which means that its discourse of "goodness" and "gentleness," whose role in everyday life as a tool of female pedagogical influence has been shown, formed part of a literary convention as well. In the vast majority of poems and novels, it was the type of speech attributed to women, who were idealized to the extent of mawkishness as the guardians of human sympathy and purer feeling, companions, pure souls, bearers of solace.[32]

One more literary device is thrown into relief by the two passages in juxtaposition. As a literary stock-in-trade, both endings attain (or enforce) closure, which in recent years has been studied in Victorian classic realism in general.[33] In *Black Beauty* closure is at least twofold. For one thing its ending, like that of *David Copperfield,* suggests that there exists a sacred domestic space tended by an Angel in the House (or rather, three), a refuge from a world of contingency and menace painted in lurid enough detail, and that this shelter will end only with death. Secondly, closure is suggested by a final distinct marking of one of the contending discourses as privileged. In Black Beauty's "last home" (as already shortly before in the temperance lady's exhortations to the carter), horse language is now spoken by humans:

> The younger lady . . . took to me very much; she said . . . I had such a good face.

Obviously this does not mean breed or pliability, but goodness of heart.

Conclusion

"It would never have enter'd my mind, I vow,
To find such a deal in nothing."
                    —Lytton, *"The Eagle and His Companions"*

Aᴛ the end of this study, at least one moral may "adorn the tale" that has been told. The quest for the English fable in the nineteenth century has proved the truth of the old adage that those live longest who were once reported dead. Lord Lytton, of course, would give a different reason for the same evidence: Aesop, never having been born, he never hath died.

The age abounded in fables—whether as short, pragmatic texts, as emblematic "typological" poems, as their increasingly skeptical pastiches, or as self-deconstructing antifables leading to aporia. Numberless poems that used fable motifs served to provide edification and exhortation, amusement and erotic innuendo. In prose fables bees were among the busiest in carrying edifying (and politically correct) messages, and even canvassed for temperance, while Aesop was harnessed to religious controversy as well as party politics.

In the hands of skilled versifiers and ingenious illustrators, the fable became an intellectual game but never quite lost its capacity to highlight man's shortcomings and life's ironies. By various means fable authors multiplied the meanings of their texts so that stable truth began to appear fragile or even self-defeating, and timeless wisdom was made a mere pretext for more topical insights. Novels and romances incorporated fable structures, but where the larger narrative mold was made complex enough to confront and destabilize different ways of making sense of the world, the traditional parabolic movement from a stereotype through a recognition of its doubtful character to deeper understanding and insight seemed no longer very helpful and was at best, in the form of short insets, built into what amounted to a mere configuration of possible views.

The critic who, in 1874, first pointed out that the fable had finally evolved into a "serious" literary form capable of ambiguity or even indeterminacy deserves a final honorary mention. Two small volumes from Robert Louis Stevenson's own hand called *Moral Emblems* have become rare collector's items; a third volume, just as valuable, bears the title *The Graver and the Pen.* Stevenson manufactured them in 1882 together with his twelve-year-old stepson, and illustrated them with woodcuts of more than rugged charm. The Pentland Edition of Stevenson's *Works* presents them under the heading of "Stevenson at Play." The books contain parodies of emblematic fables—complete with picturae, thus true to tradition. "The Disputatious Pines," from *The Graver and the Pen,* may serve, I think, as a fit emblem to conclude the preceding discussion of the age and permanence of the fable. The infinite fatigue of two bickering pines with which Stevenson's mock fable ends can be read as a satirical comment on the genre, which will probably continue to "be here" even though, in all fairness, it may often be considered more soporific than sapient:[1]

The Disputatious Pines

The first pine to the second said:
"My leaves are black, my branches red;
I stand upon this moor of mine,
A hoar, unconquerable pine."

The second sniffed and answered: "Pooh,
I am as good a pine as you."

"Discourteous tree," the first replied,
"The tempest in my boughs has cried,
The hunter slumbered in my shade,
A hundred years ere you were made."

The second smiled as he returned:
"I shall be here when you are burned."

So far dissension ruled the pair,
Each turned to each a frowning air,
When flickering from the bank anigh,
A flight of martens met their eye.
Some time their course they watched;
                              and then
They nodded off to sleep again.

R. L. Stevenson, "The Disputatious Pines" from _The Graver and the Pen_

Notes

Preface

1. The book referred to is Horst Dölvers, *Robert Louis Stevenson. Interpretationen* (Berne: Francke, 1969). The articles are listed in the bibliography. The quotation from Edward Robert Bulwer, earl of Lytton, is from his *Fables in Song*, 2d ed., 2 vols. (Leipzig: Tauchnitz, 1874), I:15–16. See below chapter 5, "Setting the stage."

Introduction: The Fable of the Fable's Death

1. Cf. H. Steers in his dedication to R. B. Sheridan: "Though fables' prodigies, are o'er, / Yet will thy classic mind explore / The glowing tints by time convey'd / And morals lurking in the shade." *Aesop's Fables, New Versified from the Best English Editions* (Hull: Printed for the Author, 1803), 51.

2. Nicolas Bentley, *The Victorian Scene* (London: Weidenfeld & Nicolson, 1968); R. D. Altick, *Victorian People and Ideas* (London: Dent, 1973); Alan Delgado, *Victorian Entertainment* (Newton Abbot: David & Charles, 1971) and Patrick Beaver, *The Spice of Life. Pleasures of the Victorian Age* (London: Elm Tree Books, 1979). As for bibliographies, there is, for instance, no entry "fable" under "genre" in Harris W. Wilson and Diane Long Hoeveler, *English Prose and Criticism in the Nineteenth Century. A Guide to Information Sources* (Detroit: Gale Research, 1979).

3. Lothar Hönnighausen, *Präraphaeliten und Fin de Siècle. Symbolistische Tendenzen in der englischen Spätromantik* (München: Fink, 1991, UTB 1630). Parables as a subclass of fables are discussed later in the introduction.

4. Quoted from M. E. Smith: "A fable is a short tale, obviously false, devised to impress by the symbolic representation of human types, lessons of expediency and morality." "The Fable and Kindred Forms," *Journal of English and Germanic Philology* 14 (1915): 529.

5. Thomas Noel, *Theories of the Fable in the Eighteenth Century* (New York and London: Columbia University Press, 1975), 145–54. The functions of the fable in eighteenth-century England are discussed extensively in S. H. Daniel, "Political and Philosophical Uses of Fables in Eighteenth-Century England," *The Eighteenth Century: Theory and Interpretation* 23 (1982); 151–71. See also for France Friederike Hassauer, *Die Philosophie der Fabeltiere* (München: Fink, 1986).

6. Daniel, "Political and Philosophical Uses," 171.

7. Harald Weinrich, "Wenn Ihr die Fabel vertreibt," in *Information und Imagination*, edited by the Bayerische Akademie der Wissenschaften (München: Piper, 1973), 70 and 61–62 (my translation).

8. Ariane Neuhaus-Koch in Peter Hasubeck, ed., *Fabelforschung.* (Darmstadt: Wissenschaftliche Buchgesellschaft, 1983), 184. See also Hasubeck, *Die Fabel. Theorie, Geschichte und Rezeption einer Gattung* (Berlin: Schmidt, 1982). According to the latter monograph, Pack Carnes's bibliography *Fable Scholarship,* and more recent bibliographical sources, detailed studies of nineteenth-century fables have so far been restricted to German speaking countries. For Hey, Haug, Busch and others, there is a good survey in Reinhardt Dithmar, *Die Fabel. Geschichte, Struktur, Didaktik* (Paderborn: Schöningh, 7, 1988), 114–23 and 228. Pauline Schanz, whose *101 neue Fabeln* were illustrated by Fedor Flinzer, is a trouvaille in Doderer, Klaus, *Fabeln. Formen, Figuren, Lehren* (München: dtv, 1977). As for the fable in Russia, Lidija Vindt mentions a program "Back to Aesop!" and a "blossoming of the four-line fable" in the form of the epigram around 1825. Lidija Vindt, "Die Fabel als literarisches Genre," *Poetica* 9 (1977): 108–9.

9. Max Plessow, *Geschichte der Fabeldichtung in England* (Berlin: Mayer & Müller, 1906); Edward Hodnett, *Aesop in England. The Transmission of Motifs in Seventeenth Century Illustrations of Aesop's Fables* (Charlottesville, Va.: University Press of Virginia, 1979); Smith, "Notes on the Rimed Fable," 206–16. Hermann Lindner notes "an excessive backlog in research on English fables" in his *Fabeln der Neuzeit: England, Frankreich und Deutschland. Ein Lese-und Arbeitsbuch* (München: Fink, 1978), 45. In his anthology France is represented with fable poetry of 1801, 1840, 1860, 1854, and 1855. Germany features even more extensively with Haug, Grillparzer, Heine, Fröhlich, Hey, and with texts from Schopenhauer's *Parerga und Paralipomena.* H. J. Blackham, in his book *The Fable as Literature* (London: Athlone Press, 1985), 127, restricts himself, as far as the nineteenth century is concerned, to a note on the spiritual affinity of Samuel Butler's *The Way of All Flesh* with Aesop and La Fontaine.

10. Lytton, Edward Robert Bulwer, Earl of, *Fables in Song,* 2 vols.([2] Leipzig: Tauchnitz, 1874), 1:14.

11. See Renate v. Heydebrand, "Parabel, Geschichte eines Begriffs zwischen Rhetorik, Poetik und Hermeneutik," *Archiv für Begriffsgeschichte,* 34 (1991): 120. Elm's and Hasubek's discussion of V. Heydebrandt's article in relation to Johann Gottfried Herder is the basis of my free translation. Theo Elm and Peter Hasubek, eds., *Fabel und Parabel. Kulturgeschichtliche Prozesse im achtzehnten Jahrhundert* (München: Fink, 1994), 8.

12. Judges 9:8–20, 2 Kings 14:9–10. See Dithmar, *Die Fabel,* 214 and Annabel Patterson, *Fables of Power. Aesopian Writing and Political History* (Durham, N.C., London: Duke University Press, 1991), 3–4. On Mandeville and Toland I follow Daniel, 159 and 156.

13. See below, chapter 3.

14. To understand Elm's use of "parable" it should be borne in mind that German has a different word (Gleichnis) for the parables of the New Testament. The wish to restrict the meaning of the term parable to the latter sense obviously deprived Stevenson of *le mot juste* for the distinctive contemporary structure that he wished to describe (see below, chapter 5, and notes). In our days Dithmar (*Die Fabel,* 165–71, 180, 184), quoting Grimm ("a fable is a parable and a parable is a fable," *Deutsches Wörterbuch,* vol. 8, 1889), subsumes fables, parables, and Gleichnisse under one category ("parabolische oder gleichnishafte Rede"), distinct from exempla (with only one content level) and allegories (which are dark in the beginning and need deciphering). To specify traditional fables (Phaedrus, Avianus etc.), I shall use the term apologues.

15. The quotations given are from Lytton, *Fables in Song* (see below, chapter 5); George Macdonald, "Sir Lark and King Sun," (in E. Davenport, ed., *Story Poems for Young and Old* [London: Cassell, 1891], see below, chapter 1); and R. L. Stevenson, "Lord Lytton's *Fables in Song*" (*Works*, Pentland Edition, edited by Edmund Gosse, Vol. 20 [London: Cassell, 1907], see below, chapter 5).

CHAPTER 1. HUMOR, SATIRE, EDUCATION

1. (Elizabeth Sandham, ed.), *Claris de Florian. Select Fables* (London: Harris, 1806); Lewis Jackson, ed., *Fables de Florian* (London: 1837) and *Jean Pierre Florian's Fables* (London: Law, 1851); Charles Yeld, ed., *Florian's Fables* (London: Macmillan, 1888); Philip Perring, *The Fables of Florian, Done into English Verse* (London: Longman, 1896).

2. Robert Henryson, *The Poems and Fables of Robert Henryson ... Collected ... by D. Laing* (Edinburgh: W. Paterson, 1865); *Krilof and His Fables*, Translated by W. R. S. Ralston (London: Strahan, 1869); Thomas Bewick, *The Works of Thomas Bewick* (Newcastle: Charnley, 1820) and *Bewick's Select Fables of Aesop and Others* (London: Bickers and Son, 1886); Job Crithannah (pseud.), *Fifty-one Original Fables ... with Eighty-Five Original Designs by R. Cruikshank* (London: Hamilton, Adams & Co., 1833); W. B. Le Gros, *Fables and Tales, Suggested by the Frescos of Pompeii and Herculaneum. Twenty Engraved Plates by F. Bromley* (London: R. Bentley, 1835); *The Fables of Pilpay. Cuts by A. R. Branston* (London: Baldwin, Cradock, & Joy, 1818) and *The Morall Philosophie of Doni. (Translated) by Sir Thomas North* (London: D. Nutt, 1888). For Bidpai see specifically Barbara Quinnam, *Fables from Incunabula to Modern Picture Books. A Selective Bibliography* (Washington: Library of Congress, 1966), 16–30. For reeditions of older collections see, for example, *The English Catalogue of Books. Books Issued in the United Kingdom of Great Britain and Ireland 1801–1836* and *Index to the British Catalogue of Books Published During the Years 1837–1857, 1856–1874, 1874–80,* and *1881–89.*

3. James Northcote, *One Hundred Fables, Original and Selected* (London: Lawford, 1828). The quotation is from p. ii; the illustration of "The Lobsters" is reproduced from p. 96. Crowquill's illustration is reproduced from (Julia Corner), *Familiar Fables: In Easy Language, Suited to the Juvenile Mind* (London: Dean and Son, 1854), 50.

4. *Famous Fables in Modern Verse* (London and Edinburgh: Nelson, 1865), vi.

5. Brooke Boothby, *Fables and Satires* (Edinburgh: Constable, 1809). v.

6. (Samuel Croxall), *Fables of Aesop and Others: Newly Done into English, With an Application to Each Fable* (London: Tonson & Watts, 1722), 225. See also S. H. Daniel, "Political and Philosophical Uses of Fables in Eighteenth-Century England," *The Eighteenth Century: Theory and Interpretation* 23 (1982): 157.

7. Ibid., 154.

8. Annabel Patterson, *Fables of Power. Aesopian Writing and Political History* (Durham, N.C., London: Duke University Press, 1991), 150.

9. This and the next two quotes are from G. F. Townsend, *Fables of Aesop, with New Applications, Morals, etc.* (London: Warne, 1866), 80 and 124.

10. Northcote, *One Hundred Fables,* 98.

11. See Isobel Spencer, *Walter Crane* (London: Vista, 1975), 114–15, with

a photograph of an Aesopian frieze in the Villa Ionides, No. 1 Holland Park, London. Cf. also Anne S. Hobbs, ed., *Fables* (London: Victoria & Albert Museum, 1986), 108.

12. Raymond Slack, *English Pressed Glass 1830–1900* (London: Barrie & Jenkins, 1987), 57–59; and C. R. Lattimore, *English Nineteenth-Century Press-Moulded Glass* (London: Barrie & Jenkins, 1979), 52–54, both with illustrations.

13. Exhibit description in the Victoria and Albert Museum: "Screen, English, 1870–1871. Designed by Sir Laurence Alma-Tadema (1836–1912). Painted by Alma-Tadema and Laura Epps (1852–1909). Wood, painted canvas and wallpaper . . . Unfinished . . . Depicts the Epps family at dinner . . . Abandoned when the artist married in July 1871." Photograph by Helga Schwarz, Ratzeburg.

14. John Holloway and Joan Black, *Later English Broadside Ballads,* Vol. 2 (London: Routledge & Kegan Paul, 1979), 138.

15. Most of the texts in this and the following section were widely known because they were printed over and over again in anthologies, which in their turn normally went through several editions. I quote from copies of these anthologies in the British Library. On the source material, see Sabine Haass, *Gedichtanthologien der viktorianischen Zeit. Eine buchgeschichtliche Untersuchung zum Wandel des literarischen Geschmacks* (Nürnberg: Carl, 1986).

Summary reference for the quotations in this section: Thomas Moore, "The Donkey and His Panniers" and R. W. Emerson, "Talents differ" (from "The Mountain and the Squirrel"), *The Book of Humorous Poetry. With Illustrations by Charles A. Doyle* (Edinburgh: Nimmo, 1867), 116–17 and 436; Charles Mackay, "The Beauty and the Bee," W. H. Wills, ed., *Poets' Wit and Humour* (London: Bell & Daldy, 1860), 261–62; Thomas Love Peacock, "He remembered too late" (from "The Priest and the Mulberry Tree"), *Crotchet Castle,* chapter 28, David Garnett, ed., *The Novels of Thomas Love Peacock* (London: Hart-Davis, 1948), 759; J. R. Planché, "A Literary Squabble," A. H. Miles, ed., *The Poets and the Poetry of the Nineteenth Century,* vol. 10 (London: Routledge, 1907), 222–24; Robert Burns, "When up they gat" (from "The Twa Dogs"), James Kinsley, ed., *The Poems and Songs of Robert Burns,* vol. 1 (Oxford: Clarendon Press, 1968), 145; Lewis Carroll, "But the snail replied" (from "The Mock Turtle's Song"), Martin Gardner, ed., *The Annotated Alice* (Harmondsworth: Penguin, 1970), 134; E. R. Bulwer, Earl of Lytton, "Tho' life I spend," *Fables in Song,* 2nd edition (Leipzig: Tauchnitz, 1874), 1:233; Carroll, "The Lobster trims his belt," *The Annotated Alice,* 139; Lytton, "And made for himself," *Fables in Song,* 1:27; Carroll, "But the Butcher" (from "The Hunting of the Snark"), Alexander Woolcott, ed., *The Complete Works of Lewis Carroll* (London: Nonesuch Press, 1939), 689.

16. See Edward Hodnett, *Francis Barlow, First Master of English Book Illustration* (London: Scolar Press, 1978), 145–53.

17. See Daniel, "Political and Philosophical Uses," 155.

18. The title is, of course, a gibe at one of the most active educational organizations of the time, *The* Society for the Diffusion of Useful Knowledge.

19. L. J. Burpee, "Literary Piracy," *Queen's Quarterly* 46 (1939): 296–303, specifically 302.

20. See below, chapter 4, "Hypertexts."

21. Summary reference for the quotations in this section:
Boothby, *Fables and Satires,* 208; Richard Gurney, *Fables on Men and Man-*

ners (London: Davison, 1809), xii, 10–12; Thomas Moore, "For even soldiers" (from *Fables for the Holy Alliance*), Hermann Lindner, *Fabeln der Neuzeit: England, Frankreich und Deutschland.* (Munich: Fink, 1978), 86; "He put it out," *Fables and Poems by T.,* (London: Saunders, Otley, and Co., 1861), 3–4; "But surely all," *Aesop in Downing Street,* (London: Roake & Varty, 1831), 9–10; "Grey replied" and "Remember," Francis Fitz-Aesop (pseud.), *Fables of the Day* (London: Maunder, 1831), 60, 99; Lytton, "Priviledge, Patronage," *Fables in Song,* 1:192; "There is a land" (from "The Horse Resolved to Be Free"), *Aesop Junior in America* (New York: Day, 1834), 227; G. W. Carryl, "I fear appendicitis" and "used to say," *Fables for the Frivolous* (London and New York: Harper & Bros., 1898), 5, 15–16; H. C. Bennett, *The Fables of Aesop and Others Translated into Human Nature* (London: W. Kent, 1857), 15. Caldecott's drawings appeared in *The English Illustrated Magazine* (1883–84), 228–29. On Caldecott, see Simon Houfe, *The Dictionary of British Book Illustrators and Caricaturists* (Woodbridge, Suff.: Antique Collectors' Club, 1978), 189–91. On Tenniel, see Houfe, *Dictionary,* 64. J. A. Shepherd's caricature appeared in *The Strand Magazine,* 10 (1895): 235. On Shepherd, see a biographical note in *The Strand Magazine,* 10 (1895): 787 and Brigid Peppin / Lucy Micklethwait, *Dictionary of British Book Illustrators, The Twentieth Century* (London: Murray, 1983), 274. "Wheels and Woes," No. 3, in *Fables and Fancies* (London: Maxwell, 1884), n. p.

22. Summary reference for the quotations in this section: J. A. Froude, *The Cat's Pilgrimage,* in *Short Studies on Great Subjects,* vol. 1 (London: Longman, 1886), 428 (my italics); Northcote, "Then let us all unite," *One Hundred Fables,* 79; Lytton, "Why dost thou so," in E.[sic] Davenport, ed., *Story Poems for Young and Old* (London: Cassell, 1891), 6; E. L. Aveline, "The difficulty" and "O! Edward, hide that foolish face" from "Advertisement," *The Mother's Fables in Verse,* 10; George Macdonald, "Glorious was she" (from "Sir Lark and King Sun"), Davenport, ed., *Story Poems,* 230; "Said the young one," *Fables in Prose and Verse* (London: Burns, 1843), 5; "But soon his anger" (from "Nanny Goat"), Wilhelm Hey, *Picture Fables* (London: Routledge 1858), 61; Jane and Anne Taylor, "Take a seat," *Original Poems for Infant Minds. By Several Young Persons* (London, 1805), 2:53; R. S. Sharpe, "Who said, 'Is it you?'," *Old Friends in a New Dress; or, Familiar Fables in Verse* (London: Harvey & Darton, 1820), 32; Walter Crane, "So awkward, so shambling," *The Baby's Own Aesop* (London: Warne, 1887), 34; Jefferys Taylor, "Said the bird," *Aesop in Rhyme* (London: Baldwin, Cradoch and Joy, 1823), 63; "Said, 'This is not nice,'" *Fables in Verse, A Book for the Young* (London: Nelson, 1868), 9; Crane, "Ass judged he was scared," *The Baby's Own Aesop,* 52.

23. See the introductory chapter. In sketching this evolution of the fable genre I follow Daniel, "Political and Philosophical Uses," 170–71, who, as mentioned in the introduction, regards it as one of the explanations of the genre's "decline" in the later eighteenth century.

24. It has to be remembered, of course, that aristocratic readers of fables in the vernacular had always been very young. La Fontaine's fables of 1668 had been dedicated to Louis XIV when he was six or seven years old, Croxall's fables (1722) to the five-year-old Baron Halifax, and Gay (1727) had written for the little Duke of Cumberland.

The last title, by 'Mary Godolphin' (i.e. Lucy Aikin), teaches Pitman's 'stenographic soundhand' and is not to be confused with any of the large number of primers like the tremendously popular one by Sarah Trimmer, *Ladder to*

Learning . . . A Collection of Fables . . . by Mrs. T. (about 1790), which had gone through its sixteenth edition by 1841.

25. Maria Verch, *Das englische Gedicht für Kinder vom 17. bis 20. Jahrhundert. Typen, Themen, Motive* (Heidelberg: Winter, 1983), 92–93 (my translation).

26. On Edward Lear see Vivien Noakes, *Edward Lear, 1812–1888,* Royal Academy of Arts Catalogue (London: Weidenfeld & Nicolson, 1985), 167–170. On the history of the limerick and its unknown origin see Cyril Bibby, *The Art of the Limerick* (London: Research Publishing, 1978).

CHAPTER 2. EMBLEMATICS AND *VERS DE SOCIÉTÉ*

1. William Wordsworth, "To the Same Flower" (following "To the Daisy"), *The Poetical Works,* edited by Ernest de Selincourt, 2nd edition (Oxford: Clarendon Press, 1952), 138. The typological poetry of the nineteenth century (excluding fable-related material) is extensively treated in Hönnighausen's monograph mentioned in the Introduction.

2. Hermann Tiemann, "Wort und Bild in der Fabeltradition bis zu La Fontaine," in *Buch und Welt,* Festschrift for Gustav Hofmann, edited by Hans Striedl and others (Wiesbaden: Harrassowitz, 1965), 237–60. For an extensive discussion of Corrozet's emblematic use of traditional fables see Barbara Tiemann's monograph *Fabel und Emblem. Gilles Corrozet und die französische Renaissance-Fabel* (München: Fink, 1974). Cf. also Mason Tung, "Fables in Emblems," *Studies in Iconography* 12 (1988): 43–60 (a study of Peacham's *Minerva Britanna*).—Emblematic fables are discussed extensively in chapter 7, "Late Emblematics." The illustration from Corrozet's *Hecatomgraphie* (Paris, 1543, sheet H 5 v, H 6 r, copy: Bayerische Staatsbibliothek München) is reproduced from Tiemann's article.

3. Geffrey Whitney, *A Choice of Emblemes* (orig. Leyden, 1585), edited by Henry Green (New York: Blom, Benjamin, 1967), 147 and 40.

4. John Bunyan, *A Book for Boys and Girls, The Miscellaneous Works of John Bunyan,* edited by Roger Sharrock (Oxford: Clarendon Press, 1980), 6: 224. Johann Abricht (i.e., Jonathan Birch), "Vain, foolish youth!" *Divine Emblems* (London: T. Ward, 1838), 54.

5. Albrecht Schöne, *Emblematik und Drama im Zeitalter des Barocks,* 2nd edition (München: Beck, 1968), 49–50. See also Monika Hueck, *Textstruktur und Gattungssystem* (Kronberg/T.: Scriptor, 1975), 104–11, here 109–10. The influence of the emblem on the *illustrators* of Gay is discussed by S. G. Huete, "John Gay's Fables I and II: A Study in the 18th Century Fable" (Univ. of S. Miss. Dissertation, 1973), 31–59. For a hypothesis concerning the fable's "two perspectives" on order, see chapter 6, "Levels of Verisimilitude."

6. Jean de La Fontaine, *Fables,* in *Œuvres complètes,* edited by René Groos and Jacques Schiffrin (Paris: Gallimard 1954), 1:250 (Book X, Fable 6).

7. The following excerpts are from Patrick Brontë, *Cottage Poems* (Halifax: Holden, 1811), 105–109.

8. On "decoding" and "deciphering" in traditional and original fables, see chapter 6, "Levels of Verisimilitude," and note.

9. Brontë, *Cottage Poems,* vii–viii.

10. Lytton, "Fool! Thy good fortune" (from "A Provision for Life") and "Over the depth" (from "Composure"), *Fables in Song* 1:55, 99.

11. Some information on trivial songs and royalty ballads under Victoria is

found in Arthur Jacobs's article "The British Isles," in Denis Stevens, ed., *A History of Song* (London: Hutchinson, 1960), 124–80 and in Geoffrey Bush's chapter "Songs" in *Music in Britain: The Romantic Age 1800–1914*, edited by Nicholas Temperley (London: Athlone, 1981), 266–87.

Just as with *vers de société*, there is no comprehensive account of the "drawing room effusions" of Victorian composers, whose only earnings were often from settings of "songs" and "ballads." Bush mentions the renowned Alexander Mackenzie (who set Tennyson's "What does little birdie say?") and the something like 300 songs by Frederic Cowen ("Golden Glories"). As in the case of the settings by A. G. Thomas ("Time's Garden"), the general impression would have been "elegant, sensuous, feminine—the sort of music Massenet might have written" (Bush, 280–82). Jacobs gives as examples the texts and compositions by Thomas Moore (like "The Last Rose of Summer," which Moore set to music himself) and mentions the names of, among others, John Stevenson and Henry Bishop ("Home, sweet home"), C. E. Horn ("Cherry ripe"), J. L. Hatton, J. P. Knight, Henry Russell, Arthur Sullivan ("The Lost Chord"), and Edward German ("The English Rose").

Gabriel Fauré's "Le Papillon et la fleur" can be heard, interpreted by Janet Baker, on compact disk (Hyperion Records, CD A 66320).

12. Summary reference for the quotations in this section:

Lytton, "The green," "And the branches," "All in a flutter," "Which in haste," *Fables in Song,* 1:18, 2:256, 1:243, 1:48; Philip Bourke Marston, "The Rose and the Wind," in J. L. Gilder, ed., *Representative Poems of Living Poets. American and English* (London: Cassell, 1886), 469–70; Joseph Skipsey, "The Bee and the Rose" and "Daffodil and Daisy," in A. H. Miles, ed., *The Poets and the Poetry of the Nineteenth Century* (London: Routledge, 1905), 5:571, 572; Austin Dobson, "A Fancy From Fontenelle," Miles, ed., *The Poets and the Poetry,* 6:416.

13. Walter Crane, *Flora's Feast* (London: Cassell, 1889), n. p.

14. In 1880, W. D. Adams, in the introduction to his anthology *Songs of Society from Anne to Victoria* (London: Pickering, 1880), defined *society verse* as "everything . . . that is not either broadly humorous or highly imaginative in character," that is, showing a modicum of refinement, while remaining well below the standards of 'high' poetry (xiii).

15. For an analysis of fable structure see chapter 6, "Levels of Verisimilitude." For plot structure, cf., among others, Lidija Vindt, "Die Fabel als literarisches Genre," *Poetica* 9 (1977), 99–101.

CHAPTER 3. VERSE FABLES BETWEEN PIETY AND SKEPTICISM

1. See chapter 5, "The Concept of the 'Post-Darwinian Fable.'"

2. Ibid. An additional aspect of Stevenson's use of "creativity," i.e., indeterminacy, is discussed in chapter 6.

3. William Wordsworth, "To the Same Flower." See above chapter 2, "Fable Material in Emblematic Poetry." Cf. Rachel Trickett, "Cowper, Wordsworth, and the Animal Fable," *Review of English Studies* 34 (1983): 471–80.

4. Summary reference for the quotations in this section:

Wordsworth, "Frail is the bond" (from "The Oak and the Broom"), *The Poetical Works,* 1:132, 134; William Blake, "I am set to light the ground" (from "A Dream"), *William Blake's Writings,* edited by G. E. Bentley, Jr. (Oxford: Clarendon Press, 1978), 49; Percy Bysshe Shelley, "The Sensitive Plant," *Poeti-*

cal Works, edited by Thomas Hutchinson, 2nd edition (London: Oxford University Press, 1970), 589–96; Charles Harpur, "The blessing craved" (from "The Cloud"), in Miles, ed., *The Poets and the Poetry of the Nineteenth Century,* 4:561; Richard Chenevix Trench, "Such chalices" (from "The Falcon's Reward"), in Davenport, ed., *Story Poems for Young and Old,* 232; Trench, "Leaving all listening spirits" (from "The Monk and the Bird"), in F. N. Paton, ed., *Bards and the Birds* (London: Reeves & Turner, 1894), 21: Trench, "I felt my thoughts" (from "The Sparrow and the Caged Bird"), in Davenport, ed., *Story Poems for Young and Old,* 235; Elizabeth Barrett Browning, "While we are thinking earthly things" (from "The Poet and the Bird. A Fable"), *The Poetical Works* (London: Frowde, 1904), 278; Alfred Austin, "If God / Be God" (from "The Owl and the Lark"), in Paton, ed., *Bards and the Birds,* 395–400; Lytton, "Measure thy being's depth" and "The conscious waters" (from "The Rainpool"), "Hope's sorceries" (from "Sic Itur"), *Fables in Song* 1:142, 1:107 (my italics); Thomas Hardy, "Laws ... which say" (from "The Subalterns"), *The Complete Poetical Works of Thomas Hardy,* edited by Samuel Hynes (Oxford: Oxford University Press, 1982), 1:155.

5. Jürgen Link and Wulf Wülfing, eds., *Bewegung und Stillstand in Metaphern und Mythen. Fallstudien zum Verhältnis von elementarem Wissen und Literatur im 19. Jahrhundert* (Stuttgart: Klett-Cotta, 1984). See chapter 8, "Second Formation of Discourses—Traditional Morals vs. Pragmatics," near the end.

6. Matthew Arnold, *The Complete Prose Works of Matthew Arnold,* edited by R. H. Super (Ann Arbor: University of Michigan Press, 1968), 5: 142–43.

Chapter 4. "Thank God There Are No Wolves in England!"—Fables in Prose

1. Summary reference for the quotations in this section:
"Edward Baldwin" (i.e., William Godwin), "If we would benefit" and "In the last fable," *Fables Ancient and Modern, Adapted for the Use of Children, from Three to Eight Years of Age* (London: Hodgkins, 1805), iii and 93; Corner, "The desire of vying," *Familiar Fables,* 51; Northcote, "You are both right," *One Hundred Fables,* 45; Corner, "(You) both are wrong," *Familiar Fables,* 27; "How dismal you look," *The Leisure Hour* No. 775 (November 1866): 703; Elizabeth Sandham, "One whole day in gathering wax," *The Perambulations of a Bee and a Butterfly* (London: Lewis, 1812), 129; "Sister, sister," *Instructive Fables for Christian Scholars. By the Author of "The Last Day of the Week"* (i.e., Eliza Cheap, London: Seeley, 1834), 11; Isaac Watts, "In works of labour," (from "Against Idleness and Mischief"), *Divine Songs Attempted in Easy Language for the Use of Children,* 1st edition (1715), in *The Works of the English Poets,* edited by Alexander Chalmers (London: J. Johnson and others, 1810), 2: 91; William Hogarth, *Industry and Idleness Exemplified* (1747), in *Hogarth Illustrated,* edited by John Ireland (London, 1791): I, 190; "There were two bees," *Fables for the Nursery* (London: Harris, 1824), 42, 49; "The Bee worked day after day," *Fables and True Stories of Children,* 11th edition (London: Varty, 1855), 31; Ingram Cobbin, "The drones," *Moral Fables and Parables* (London: Westley & Davis, 1832), 40–1; Margaret Gatty, "Don't you see," "You make me young again," "It is very easy to ridicule," *Parables From Nature* (1st edition 1855–1871; London: Bell, 1880), 14, 363, 29–30; Arthur Kelly,

"The Rosebud loved," *The Rosebud and Other Tales. Pictured by Walter Crane* (London: Fisher Unwin, 1909), 14.

2. Robert Gittings and J. Manton, *Claire Clairmont and the Shelleys 1789–1879* (Oxford: Oxford University Press, 1992), 7.

3. For Corner's revisions, see chapter 1.

4. See chapter 8, "Subformation of Discourses (Exhortation): 'Influence,'" about Stephen Mintz's monograph *A Prison of Expectations. The Family in Victorian Culture* (New York, London: New York University Press, 1983).

5. See chapter 1, "Continuities."

6. Summary reference for the quotations in this section:
Anne Jane Cupples, "Instead of drawing the moral," and "Poor Grace was reminded," *Fables Illustrated by Stories From Real Life* (London: Nelson, 1874), 20, 22. Ms. Cupples was the author of widely read educational romances with titles like *Alice Leighton; or, A Good Name is Rather to Be Chosen Than Riches* (1869). Randolph Caldecott, *Some of Aesop's Fables with Modern Instances Shewn in Designs by Randolph Caldecott* (London: Macmillan, 1883), 3, 15; Gregson Gow, "With spasmodic strength," *New Light Through Old Windows* (London: Blackie, 1883), 63–80; 'Arthur Wallbridge' (i.e., W. A. B. Lunn), "To gain the best fruits" (from "The Wise Fool"), *Bizarre Fables* (London: Orr, 1842), 26. For Froude, *The Cat's Pilgrimage* see chapter 1 and note.

7. Detlev Gohrbandt discusses this juxtaposition of "primary" and "secondary illustrations" in the teaching of English as a foreign language. ("Zur Semantik und Didaktik der Fabel: Bild und Text bei James Northcote und Randolph Caldecott," *Die neueren Sprachen* 91 (1992): 605–7.

8. Gérard Genette, *Palimpsestes—La Littérature au second degré* (Paris: Editions du seuil, 1982), 11–64. I do not accept Genette's use of the term parody, however, which is highly idiosyncratic.

9. Nina Auerbach and U. C. Knoepflmacher, eds., *Forbidden Journeys: Fairy Tales and Fantasies by Victorian Women Writers* (Chicago, London: University of Chicago Press, 1992), 321.

10. Summary reference for the quotations in this section:
John Collinson, "He dipped his proboscis," *Fables, Dedicated to Temperance Societies. By a Durham Clergyman.* (London: New British Temperance Society, 1840), 9; Oliver Pacis, "Look at the Grasshopper," *Temperance Rays from Aesop's Lamp* (London: Kelly, 1900), 63–64; George Ade, "My good woman," *Fables in Slang* (London and Chicago: Pearson, 1900), 40–41; Richard Gurney, "Aesop designed his works" and "The Demagogue and the Clergyman," *Fables on Men and Manners* (London: Davison, 1809), xiii and 10–11; W. J. Linton, "I am a rough plain man," quoted from Martha Vicinus, *The Industrial Muse. A Study of Nineteenth-Century Working Class Literature* (London: Croom Helm, 1974), 117 (see following note); Walter Crane, "We can easily find details" (from "The Donkey and the Common"), *Cartoons for the Cause, 1886–1896* (Reprint London: The Journeyman Press, 1976), text following plate 11. The reproduction of Crane's "The Vampire" is taken from the same 1976 reprint, plate 3. "Aesop's Fables—Cabinet Edition" is reproduced from a broadsheet in the British Library, 188.d.3.

11. An eighteenth-century debate of long standing, cp. Daniel's report on William Shenstone and Robert Dodsley (1760), Daniel, "Political and Philosophical Uses," 164.

12. Vicinus, *The Industrial Muse,* 116.

13. See Introduction and notes above.

14. See, for instance, J. Hillis Miller, "'Hieroglyphical Truth' in *Sartor Resartus*: Carlyle and the Language of Parable," in *Victorian Perspectives: Six Essays*, edited by John Clubbe and Jerome Meckier (Newark: University of Delaware Press, 1989), 1–20; Nancy A. Metz, "Ayala's Angel: Trollope's Late Fable of Change and Choice," in *Dickens Studies Annual: Essays on Victorian Fiction* 9 (1981): 217–232; and Gillian Sheperd, "The Kailyard," in *The History of Scottish Literature*, edited by Douglas Gifford, vol. 3 (Aberdeen: Aberdeen University Press, 1988), 309–320.

15. Peter A. Dale, "George Eliot's 'Brother Jacob': Fables and the Physiology of Common Life," *Philological Quarterly* 64 (1985): 19, 30.

16. Eliot uses "parable" here in its centuries-old rhetorical meaning of *similitudo*, as preserved in theological writings (cf. Renate v. Heydebrand, "Parabel, Geschichte eines Begriffs zwischen Rhetorik, Poetik und Hermeneutik," *Archiv für Begriffsgeschichte*, 34 (1991): 118). This overlap of the meanings of parable and emblem is quite common in the nineteenth century. Cf. Darwin's frequently mentioned "Parable of the Tangled Bank" ("this view of life") at the end of *On the Origin of Species*. See Introduction and notes.

17. Barbara McGovern, "Pier Glasses and Sympathy in Eliot's *Middlemarch*," *Victorian Newsletter* 72 (1987): 6–8.

18. G. B. Shaw, *An Unsocial Socialist* (1st edition 1884; London: Virago, 1980), 214–15.

19. See Valerie Shaw, *The Short Story: A Critical Introduction* (London: Longman, 1983), 67, 73.

20. The reader is reminded of the broad meaning I give to fable throughout this study, as discussed in the Introduction and its notes, and, with reference to Stevenson, at the beginning of chapter 3. For hypertextuality, see earlier note. Aporia is discussed at the end of this chapter.

21. Lytton, *Fables in Song*, 1:56–67. I am adopting here the interpretation of Stevenson's story given by Harold Orel in *The Victorian Short Story. Development and Triumph of a Literary Genre* (Cambridge: Cambridge University Press, 1986), 119–20. Orel, however, does not mention the story's relationship with Lytton's fable.

22. See Introduction and notes above.

23. See chapter 5, "The Concept of the 'Post-Darwinian' Fable."

24. Edmund Gosse in the commentary of the *Pentland Edition* of Stevenson's works (London: Cassell, 1907), 20:323. In 1888, Stevenson promised Longman a book of fables. In Stevenson criticism, the fables are hardly ever mentioned. The quotations given here are from the *Pentland Edition*, 321–74.

25. See chapter 5, "The Concept of the 'Post-Darwinian' Fable." I pursue the following reading (like that of "The Sinking Ship") in the context of Hillis Miller's assumptions in *The Linguistic Moment. From Wordsworth to Stevens* (Princeton: Princeton University Press, 1985), 43–54.

26. Theo Elm, *Die moderne Parabel* (UTB 1630, München: Fink, 1991), 285, referring to the wider context of twentieth-century art. See also Elm, 137–38. As for modern *aporia*, cf. Franz Kafka: "There is a goal but no way" (quoted by Elm, 90).

CHAPTER 5. LORD LYTTON'S *FABLES IN SONG* (I): THE SOURCE OF R. L. STEVENSON'S THEORY OF THE NINETEENTH-CENTURY FABLE

1. R. L. Stevenson, "Lord Lytton's *Fables in Song*," in *Works*, edited by Edmund Gosse (Pentland Edition, London: Cassell, 1907), 20: 191–201. The quotations given are on pp. 191–95.

2. Morley's estimate and the biographical context of Lytton's work are given in A. B. Harlan, *Owen Meredith. A Critical Biography of Robert, First Earl of Lytton* (New York: Columbia University Press, 1946), 204. Harlan quotes from Lady Betty Balfour's edition of the *Personal and Literary Letters of Robert Lytton.*

3. I have given an account of Stevenson's life and the formation of his narrative theory in my book *Der Erzähler Robert Louis Stevenson* (Berne: Francke, 1969).

4. As has been indicated in the Introduction, English and German criticism regrettably differ on the meaning of the term parable. Stevenson conforms to English usage in giving fable a very large meaning (including what Germans would call parables such as Swift's "Fable of the Coats"), reserving parable for "the parables of the New Testament" (in German "Gleichnisse") and fumbling for paraphrases of what he wants to instate as *the contemporary fable*: "metaphysical," "indeterminate," "suggestive," "the collocation of significant facts in life, the reader being left to resolve for himself the vague, troublesome, and yet not definitely moral sentiment which has been thus created." This is basically what Theo Elm in *Die moderne Parabel* claims as features of the parable, and I am using the term parable with this meaning. See chapter 6, "Questionable Fabulation," for a detailed discussion of "the reader('s) being left to resolve for himself."

5. For Stevenson's French reading, see J. C. Furness, *Voyage to Windward. The Life of R. L. Stevenson* (London: Faber, 1952), 111–16. Ambiguity as an aesthetic value is the topic of Christoph Bode's monograph *Ästhetik der Ambiguität. Zur Funktion und Bedeutung von Mehrdeutigkeit in der Literatur der Moderne* (Tübingen: Niemeyer, 1988). For indeterminacy as a ground of literary texts cf. J. Hillis Miller, "The Search for Grounds in Literary Study," in *Rhetoric and Form. Deconstruction at Yale,* edited by R. Con Davis and Ronald Schleifer (Norman: University of Oklahoma Press, 1985), 19–35.

6. For Lytton's life, see Harlan, *Owen Meredith* and E. N. Raymond, *Victorian Viceroy. The Life of Robert, the First Earl of Lytton* (London: Regency Press, 1980). The title of Lytton's ill-considered verses is an echo of an early Tennyson poem on *religious* doubt, "Supposed Confessions of a Second-Rate Sensitive Mind." Lytton's "morbidly subjective" lines, likewise a dramatic monologue, pretend to be the thoughts of a dying poet "full of regret for unrealized hopes and shattered dreams" (Harlan, 177).

7. The quotations from Lytton's *Fables in Song* are from the Tauchnitz Edition (Leipzig: Tauchnitz, 1874). Summary reference:
"Down with it," "Aesop, never having been born," 1:7–16; "Merrily, mockingly," 1:44, "Nature hath given," 2:114; "A little child," 1:71; "Bohemian born," 1:108; "One may lose," 1:29; "Gracing our President's chair," 1:208; "Stop thy wail," 1:218; "Sage or simple," 1:220; "A Haughty Spirit," 2:175; "The Mountain and the Marsh," 2:125–36; "Thrilled (at) the contact," 2:177, "So aid me," 1:97, "But such tales as these," 2:196 (my italics); "Minds whose natural home is high," 2:121; "Low natures," 2:125; "'Tis the way," 1:209; "By merit," 1:234; "Privilege, Patronage," 1:192; "Strength to be," 1:246; "The poet's form," 2:116; "When, pausing," 2:136; "Thro' all my being," 1:178; "How admirably organized," 2:138; "Blind chance," 2:140; "Soap-boiling factory," 2:247; and "Maternal love," 2:232.

8. The illustration shows an engraving by Marcus Gheeraerts from Edewaerd de Dene, *De warachtighe Fabulen der Dieren* (Brügge: de Clerck, 1567),

which accompanies Aesop's fable of the goat outwitted by the fox, who escapes from a well by using the goat's back as a support.

9. Summary reference for the quotations in this section:
Wiliam Blake, "And did those feet" (from "Milton," 1809), *William Blake's Writings,* edited by G. E. Bentley, Jr. (Oxford: Clarendon Press, 1978), 1:318. Coleridge's text is a free version of Schiller's *Die Piccolomini* (II, iv, 123–28), in *The Complete Poetical Works of S. T. Coleridge,* edited by E. H. Coleridge (Oxford: Clarendon Press, 1912), 21:649. Cf. Douglas Bush, *Mythology and the Romantic Tradition in English Poetry,* 51–56.

10. Though I try to avoid specialized terminology in most points, the background of the following analysis is the theory of *classic realism, closure,* and *the subject in ideology* as summarized by, among others, Catherine Belsey in *Critical Practice* (London: Methuen, 1980), Colin MacCabe in *James Joyce and the Revolution of the Word* (London: Macmillan, 1978), and Rosalind Coward/John Ellis in *Language and Materialism: Developments in Semiology and the Theory of the Subject* (London: Routledge & Kegan Paul, 1977). An extensive discussion can be found in the chapter "Discourse as Subjectivity" in Antony Easthope's book *Poetry as Discourse* (London: Methuen, 1983), 30–50.

11. See Diane Macdonell, "From Ideology to Discourse: the Althusserian Stand," *Theories of Discourse, An Introduction* (Oxford: Blackwell, 1986), 24–42.

12. Scott's statement already appeared in the *Quarterly Review,* 14 (1815): 193. See Möller's recent discussion of the much-gnawed bone of realism in the interesting light that falls on it from the criticism in Early Victorian magazines (Joachim Möller, *Romankritik in Großbritannien 1800–1860. Mit einem Kapitel zum Kritikpotential der Illustration* (Anglistische Forschungen 212, Heidelberg: Winter, 1991), 157–64.

13. It has been suggested that this "natural" code goes back to medieval bestiaries and their allegorical interpretations of (variable) groups of animals subsumed under roles and functions. Cf. A. C. Henderson, "Medieval Beasts and Modern Cages: The Making of Meaning in Fables and Bestiaries," *PMLA* 97 (1982): 45.

14. For the tension between security and adventure as categories of economic behaviour see Nerlich, *Ideology of Adventure.*

15. See chapter 1, "Verse Fables of Satire and Caricature," for the context of social satire in nineteenth-century fables, and chapter 7, "The Rhetoric of Depiction (II)" and "The Rhetoric of Depiction (III)," for contemporary events and catch-phrases.

16. See Macdonell, "From Ideology to Discourse: the Althusserian Stand."

17. Wordsworth, *The Borderers,* 1515–16.

18. "Preface" to *Lyrical Ballads* (1800).

19. Cf. Darwin's discussion of "maternal love" as attributed to bees in *On the Origin of Species* (1859): "maternal love . . . is all the same to the inexorable principle of Natural Selection." *The Works of Charles Darwin,* edited by Paul H. Barrett and R. B. Freeman (London: Pickering, 1988), 145.

CHAPTER 6. LORD LYTTON'S *Fables in Song* (II): Semiotic Model and Individual Text

1. Howard Needler, "The Animal Fable among Other Medieval Literary Genres," *New Literary History* 22 (1991): 428. Peter Grzybek proposes the transla-

tion "primary" for "einfach" in Jolles's *Einfache Formen*. "Invariant Meaning Structures in Texts: Proverb and Fable," in *Issues in Slavic Literary and Cultural Theory*, edited by Karl Eimermacher, Peter Grzybek, and Georg Witte (Bochum: Brockmeyer, 1989), 350.

2. Distinguishing only two meaning levels, Hans Georg Coenen gives a linguistic account of the conditions of semantic and pragmatic well-formedness of the "Fabelzweitsinn" ("the fable's secondary meaning"). "Zur Deutbarkeit von Fabeln," *Linguistische Berichte* 4 (1976):15–21.

3. Hermann Bausinger, "Die moralischen Tiere," *Universitas* 45 (1990): 242.

4. The terminology is Jacques Lacan's, who distinguishes decoding from deciphering, i.e., "mimetic" from "linguistic" analyses of the signs of the unconscious. *Ecrits* (Paris: Editions du seuil, 1966), 269. Concerning the empirical and moral coding of the fable's agents, I differ from Klaus Grubmüller who, like Coenen, distinguishes but two "levels of isotopies" and claims that the level of the nonhuman agents is "(almost) empty of features," "without presuppositions," "merely instrumental," and thus "absolutely at disposal." "Semantik der Fabel," in *Third International Beast Epic, Fable, and Fabliau Colloquium, Münster 1979*, edited by Jan Goossens and Timothy Sodmann (Cologne: Böhlau, 1981), 133.

5. Sandham, *The Perambulations*, 129; Cobbin, *Moral Fables and Parables*, 10. See chapter 4.

6. "A butterfly, with fine painted wings," *Fables and True Stories of Children*, 11th edition (London: Varty, 1855), 30; "Ha, ha! I know of nought to beat," *Fables in Verse, A Book for the Young* (London: Nelson, 1868), 20.

7. A. C. Henderson, "Medieval Beasts and Modern Cages: The Making of Meaning in Fables and Bestiaries," *PMLA* 97 (1982): 43. Henderson sees the codes as "potential" and lays stress on their creative variation.

8. See chapter 4, "Of Bees, Butterflies, and Bookworms."

9. Needler, "The Animal Fable," 437–38.

10. Ibid., 438.

11. Lytton, "Questionable Consolation," *Fables in Song*, 2:88.

12. Needler, "The Animal Fable," 438.

13. Again, as in my reading of Stevenson's "The Sinking Ship" (see chapter 4, "Too Ambitious to Be Resumed in a Formula" and note), I refer to Hillis Miller's assumptions in *The Linguistic Moment. From Wordsworth to Stevens*. See also chapter 5, "The Concept of the 'Post-Darwinian' Fable" for a quotation of Stevenson's statement about indeterminacy.

14. Lytton, *"One wing unfinisht,"* *Fables in Song*, 2:88, "The boastful orb's last glories," ibid. 2:91, both from "Questionable Consolation."

15. See chapter 4, "Too Ambitious to Be Resumed in a Formula" and Introduction.

16. Norman Rabkin, *Shakespeare and the Problem of Meaning* (Chicago: University of Chicago Press, 1981), 33–62. The résumé is Gary Taylor's in his *Reinventing Shakespeare: A Cultural History from the Restoration to the Present* (London: Oxford University Press, 1989), 323. The chalk drawing "Grab" ("Grave," 1917) by Otto Dix is reproduced in Horst Meller, *Zum Verstehen englischer Gedichte* (Munich: Fink 1985), 29.

17. For a recent selection of literature on deconstruction, see the bibliographical entry in W. V. Harris, *Dictionary of Concepts in Literary Criticism and Theory* (New York, London: Greenwood Press, 1992), 62–63.

18. Gohrbandt, "Zur Semantik und Didaktik der Fabel," 603–4, discusses a mutual "subversion" of one of Northcote's fables and the ornamental letter (designed by William Harvey) at the fable's beginning: "There is an almost furtive dissemination of the fable's explicit meaning, a turning (trope) to an alternative one. This is what makes the fable potentially interesting and alive . . . By the supplement's subversive effects the reader is called upon to invent his own texts."

Chapter 7. Walter Crane's *The Baby's Own Aesop*—Visual Countertexts in a Victorian Picture Book

1. The full title page of the copy studied here is worth quoting for its reference to Evans's experiments in colour printing from wood engravings: Walter Crane (and Wiliam J. Linton), *The Baby's Own Aesop. Being the Fables Condensed in Rhyme. With Portable Morals Pictorially Pointed by Walter Crane. Engraved and Printed in Colours by Edmund Evans.* London: Frederick Warne and Co., Ltd. and New York (1887). Cf. for this chapter my monograph in German, *Walter Cranes Aesop. Ein viktorianisches Bilderbuch im Kontext seiner Entstehung. Buchkunst und Bilderbuch im viktorianischen England* (Kassel: Edition Reichenberger, 1994).
2. See chapter 2.
3. In my paper "Depiction vs. Picturing," I have given a more extensive discussion of my concepts of "picturing" as opposed to the "visual rhetoric of depiction," relating these concepts to the history of fable illustration (Caxton, Jacob Wolff) and the semiotic theories of Lacan, Greimas, Riffaterre, and Posner. That essay is here reduced to its empirical data. An analysis of Crane's plate "The Ass & the Sick Lion" in Lacanian terms is attempted in my paper "Gegen die Despotie der Fakten. Walter Cranes Bilderbuchphantasien zwischen Neorenaissance und Art Nouveau," in *Englische Buchillustration im europäischen Kontext,* edited by Joachim Möller (Berlin: Technische Universität, 1989), 41–55. For a general discussion of omissions and additions in book illustrations see Göran Hermerén, "Two Concepts of Illustration," in *Representation and Meaning in the Visual Arts* (Copenhagen: Scandinavian University Books, 1969), 59. Functions of illustration are discussed in J. H. Schwarcz, *Ways of the Illustrator. Visual Communication in Children's Literature* (Chicago: American Library Association, 1982), 145–49.
4. For "pointed pictorially," see the first note to this chapter. For "pictured," see Kelly, *The Rosebud and Other Tales,* title page.
5. Linton had already printed, in his Appledore Private Press, earlier versions of his limericks without illustrations (*The Wisdom of Aesop, Condensed . . . By P. J.* (Hamden, Conn.: A.A.P., 1880), which either he or Crane revised, sometimes considerably, for *The Baby's Own Aesop.* See R. M. Sills, "W. J. Linton at Yale—The Appledore Private Press," *Yale University Library Gazette,* 12 (1938): item 7.
6. For a suggestion as to the possible origin of the stanza form, see chapter 1.
7. For a history of the limerick, see Cyril Bibby, *The Art of the Limerick* (London: Research Publishing, 1978). Bibby refers to an article of 1898 in

which the term "learic" (as a portmanteau from "Lear" and "lyric") is used (p. 40).

8. For Linton's life and works, see W. J. Linton, *Memories* (London: Lawrence & Bullen, 1895) and F. B. Smith, *Radical Artisan. W. J. Linton 1812–1897* (Manchester: Manchester University Press, 1973).

9. A number of monographs on Crane have been published. The thoroughly researched account of Crane's life and works by Isobel Spencer, *Walter Crane* refers to *The Baby's Own Aesop* in merely four lines. See also M. P. Hearn, "Nursery Aesthetics: Walter Crane and his Picture Books for Children," *American Book Collector,* N.S., 2,4 (1981): 2–12 and 2,5 (1981): 19–33, and the catalogue by Greg Smith and Sarah Hyde, eds., *Walter Crane 1845–1915. Artist, Designer and Socialist* (London: Lund Humphries and Manchester: The Whitworth Art Gallery, 1989).

10. Isobel Spencer, referring to R. Schmutzler ("Blake and Art Nouveau," *The Architectural Review,* 118 (1955): 90–97), speaks of a "Proto Art Nouveau Style in England in the 1880s" in the works of Rossetti, Burne-Jones, and Crane and points to the swirling designs in Gilchrist's *Blake* as an influence on Crane. *Walter Crane* (London: Vista, 1975), 87.

11. For material on nineteenth-century techniques of color printing, see the article by Sarah Hyde in Smith and Hyde, *Walter Crane, 1845–1915.*

12. Johann Mannich, *Sacra Emblemata LXXVI in quibus summa uniuscuiusque evangeli rotunde adumbratur* (Nürnberg, 1625), 25. Reproduced from Arthur Henkel and Albrecht Schöne, eds., *Emblemata. Handbuch zur Sinnbildkunst des 16. und 17. Jahrhunderts* (Stuttgart: Metzler, 1967), col. 13.

13. Hermann Tiemann, "Wort und Bild in der Fabeltradition bis zu La Fontaine," in *Buch und Welt,* edited by Hans Striedl and others (Wiesbaden: Harrassowitz, 1965), 241. See also Barbara Tiemann, *Fabel und Emblem. Gilles Corrozet und die französische Renaissance-Fabel* (München: Fink, 1974).

14. For Corrozet, see chapter 2, "Fable Material in Emblematic Poetry."

15. H. Tiemann, "Wort und Bild," 242 and 244; Schöne, "Emblemata," 230.

16. J. Hillis Miller, "Sketches by Boz, Oliver Twist, and Cruikshank's Illustrations," in *Charles Dickens and George Cruikshank,* edited by Ada Nisbet (Los Angeles: University of California Press, 1971), 45.

17. See chapter 2, "Fable Material in Emblematic Poetry."

18. Cf. J. J. McKendry, *Aesop. Five Centuries of Illustrated Fables* (New York: Metropolitan Museum of Art, 1964).

19. Anthony Munday, *Sundry Examples* (1580), no. 78; Thomas Dekker, *The Shoemaker's Holiday* (1600), II, 3; John Gay, *The Wife of Bath* (1713), III, 1.

20. Whereas "the antique collection of greatest influence in the Middle Ages" still applies "moral categories" to Phaedrus' wolf-lamb fable, "towards the end of the twelfth century . . . fabulists (begin to) apply the ancient general lessons of weak and strong to specific classes in a real society." Henderson, "Medieval Beasts and Modern Cages," 41. See also, particularly for the sixteenth and seventeenth centuries, Patterson, *Fables of Power.*

21. "Or what man is there of you, whom if his son ask bread, will he give him a stone!" (Matth. 7:9)

22. For further details see G. D. H. Cole, *A Short History of the British Working Class Movement* (2nd edition, London: Allen & Unwin, 1948), 182, 224, 238–39. The notion of a Great Depression after 1873 is replaced by the

less dramatic one of a mere economic retardation by R. C. Floud in Floud and D. McCloskey, eds., *The Economic History of Britain Since 1700* (Cambridge, London: Cambridge University Press, 1981), 2:7. The photograph is from an album published on the occasion of Queen Victoria's jubilee, *The Queen's London. A Pictorial and Descriptive Record of the Streets, Buildings, Parks, and Scenery of the Great Metropolis* (London: Cassell, 1896), 91. Crane's fable "The Donkey and the Common," already discussed in chapter 4, is taken from Walter Crane, *Cartoons for the Cause, 1886–1989* (Reprint London: The Journeyman Press, 1976), text following plate 11.

23. Cf. Peter Grzybek, "Invariant Meaning Structures in Texts: Proverb and Fable," in *Issues in Slavic Literary and Cultural Theory*, edited by Karl Eimermacher, Peter Grzybek, and Georg Witte (Bochum: Brockmeyer, 1989), 377: "Fables incorporate no obliging rules and no 'eternal truths,' but represent models of particular circumstances . . . There are semantically contradictory fables, just as there are proverbial antonyms."

24. Hillis Miller, *The Linguistic Moment. From Wordsworth to Stevens*, 54.

25. Mikhail Bakhtin, *The Dialogical Principle*, edited by Tzvetan Todorov, Theory and History of Literature 13 (Manchester: Manchester University Press, 1984), 73.

26. Roland Posner, "What Is Culture? Toward a Semiotic Explication of Anthropological Concepts," in *The Nature of Culture*, edited by Walter A. Koch (Bochum: Brockmeyer, 1989), 240–95. Posner (p. 276) assumes that already in Baroque emblems picture and text in juxtaposition make for a deautomatization and flexibilization of culturally central (and stereotyped) codings, e.g., by "an increased awareness . . . of the possible linguistic properties of painting (division into components, their syntactic relations, etc.)." It seems to me, however, that only a parodistic handling of emblems (as in Crane's book) provides empirical evidence of this awareness.

Interestingly, Hillis Miller, in a discussion of Cruikshank's illustrations of Dickens's *Sketches by Boz* based on Gombrich, claims that "'mimetic' reading" leads to aporia. "The beholder is left face to face with the bare ink marks on the page (which) . . . constitute their own intrinsic meaning . . . (if one attempts) to identify the motifs and structuring forms which recur" (J. Hillis Miller, "Sketches by Boz, Oliver Twist, and Cruikshank's Illustrations," in *Charles Dickens and George Cruikshank*, edited by Ada Nisbet (Los Angeles: University of California Press, 1971), 52–53). On the preceding pages I have tried to describe the weak coding implied by a comparable spatial structuring in Crane's book, relating it to two possible sets of contemporary aesthetic and social signifiers.

27. Ellen Houghton's drawing was published in Walter Crane, *An Artist's Reminiscences* (London: Methuen, 1907), 277.

CHAPTER 8. "LET BEASTS BEAR GENTLE MINDS"—FABLE INTO ANIMAL BIOGRAPHY

1. Quoted in Percy Muir, *English Children's Books 1600 to 1900* (London: Batsford, 1954), 108. The illustration shows one of Walter Crane's plates to Mrs. Molesworth's *The Children of the Castle* (London, 1890). The books by Mrs. Molesworth that were illustrated by Crane are recorded in R. K. Engen, *Walter Crane as a Book Illustrator* (London: St. Martin's Press, 1975), 98–101. See also Spencer, "Appendix," in *Walter Crane*, 200–205.

2. Muir, *English Children's Books 1600 to 1900*, 108.

3. Richard Rorty, *Contingency, Irony, and Solidarity* (Cambridge: Cambridge University Press, 1989), 73–95.

4. "Meaning is always a word, expression or proposition for another word, expression or proposition and ... this transfer ... by which signifying elements are brought together so as to 'take on a meaning' cannot be predetermined by properties of the langue." "Words, expressions and propositions get their meanings from the discursive formation to which they belong." Michael Pêcheux, *Language, Semantics and Ideology: Stating the Obvious* (London: Macmillan, 1982), 188–89.

5. In using the term discourse for a value-centred coding of reality I follow Pêcheux. Cf. also Macdonell, *Theories of Discourse, An Introduction.*

6. W. Bingley, *Animal Biography* (1820). Quoted from Eric Quayle, *The Collector's Book of Children's Books* (London: Studio Vista, 1971), 51.

7. Anna Sewell, *Black Beauty: His Grooms and Companions. The Autobiography of a Horse* (1st edition 1877) (Harmondsworth: Penguin, 1954).

8. Quayle, *The Collector's Book of Children's Books*, 96. For Anna Sewell's life, see Susan Chitty, *The Woman Who Wrote Black Beauty: Anna Sewell* (London: Hodder, 1971.)

9. Anna Sewell, *Black Beauty: His Grooms and Companions*. Summary reference:
"I wish you," 11; "I have never," 12; "I never knew," 114; "We trotted up," 13; "It makes them vicious," 62; "Let us cheer up," 47; "(so we) got up our spirits," 47; "little puppies" and following, 44; "hurt my tongue," 35; "I had made up my mind," 37; "hold their heads up," 49 (italics in the text); "those horrid bits," 43; "mouth was as full," 196; "Then he must go," 200; "make old horses young," 202; "to feel quite young again," 204; "so I have nothing to fear," 208; "I wish you to pay attention" and following, 11; "I could have groaned," 105; "too much spirit to complain," 101; "Your grandmother" and following, 11; "This was the first experience," 30 (my italics); "Lift your feet" and following, 12; "The colts that live here" and following, 11, 27, 117, 12, 45; "so gentle and kind" and following, 26, 31, 101, 199; "be good and kind," 57; "Drive him gently," 114; "a quiet, humble," 31; "she'll be as good," 37; "Is he gentle?" 134–35; "quiet and pleasant," 25–26; "a sweet," 26; "fashion," 43; "What fine," 94; "a slovenly way," 112; "free from vice" and following, 36, 62; "my plan is," 200; "'tis a mockery," 165; "bad words," 45; "madly drunk," 103; "Men are strongest," 168; "If there's one devil," 180; "No one spoke," 166; "Oh! If men," 168; "I thank you," 195; "If a thing is right," 154; "And so here we are," 109; "its lifeless tongue," 168; "I am sure," 198; "My ladies have promised," 208; "The younger lady," 205.

10. Jacques Lacan, "The Mirror-Phase as Formative of the Function of the I," *New Left Review* 51 (1968): 71–77. See also *Le Seminaire de Jacques Lacan.* An accessible account of the Lancanian system is found in Wilden's translation and commentary of the *Discours de Rome* (1953) in Anthony Wilden, *The Language of the Self. The Function of Language in Psychoanalysis* (Baltimore: Johns Hopkins Press, 1968). See also Eugen Bär, "The Language of the Unconscious According to Jacques Lacan," *Semiotica* 3 (1971): 241–68 and R. C. Davis, *Lacan and Narration. The Psychoanalytic Difference in Narrative Theory* (Baltimore: Johns Hopkins, 1984).

11. Kaja Silverman, *The Subject of Semiotics* (New York, Oxford: Oxford University Press, 1983), 183; Ruth Padel, "Saddled With Ginger. Women, Men,

and Horses," *Encounter* 55 (1980): 47–54; Margaret Drabble, (ed.), *The Oxford Companion to English Literature,* 5th edition (Oxford: Oxford University Press, 1985), 888 (meanwhile corrected). Cf. Peter Reading, "Equine Feminism," *TLS,* no. 4301 (1985): 975.

12. Antony Easthope, *Poetry and Phantasy* (Cambridge: Cambridge University Press, 1989), 10–23.

13. Stephen Mintz, *A Prison of Expectations. The Family in Victorian Culture* (New York, London: New York University Press, 1983). The following paragraphs summarize Mintz, 28–39. For L. M. Child, see Mintz, 34 and 210, for Isaac Taylor, 210, for H. Humphrey, 33. For an account of a related development, see also Auerbach and Knoepflmacher, eds., *Forbidden Journeys,* 2–3: "In the 1840s and '50s, rigid didacticism had held children's fiction in thrall ... (From 1876 to 1879) children's journals that encouraged the publication of imaginative fiction began to replace the earlier magazines devoted to 'useful' moral and intellectual instruction."

14. Michel Foucault, "The Discourse on Language," in *The Archeology of Knowledge* (London: Tavistock Publications, 1972), 216–29.

15. Cf. Eph. 6:7: "with good will doing service."

16. "Industry and idleness exemplified, in the conduct of two fellow 'prentices: where the one by taking good courses ... becomes a valuable man." William Hogarth in his memoirs, see Ireland, ed., *Hogarth Illustrated,* 1:190.

17. Isaac Watts, "Against Idleness and Mischief," in *Divine Songs Attempted in Easy Language* 2:91. See chapter 4, "Of Bees, Butterflies, and Bookworms."

18. *Fables for the Nursery,* 42. See above, chapter 4. Horses, like bees, were, of course, particularly amenable to these projections due to Victorian myths about the horse as noble, willingly subservient, courageous, docile, patient, persevering, of benevolent disposition, and capable of strong attachment as well as righteous resentment of injuries. See Harriet Ritvo, *The Animal Estate. The English and Other Creatures in the Victorian Age* (Cambridge, Mass.: Harvard University Press, 1987), 19–20.

19. Michel Foucault, *Power/Discourse. Selected Interviews and Other Writings,* edited by Colin Gordon (Brighton, Sussex: The Harvester Press, 1980).

20. Following Foucault, Jürgen Link has posited a regulating principle determining "which discourses and which cultural knowledge are regarded as culturally acceptable or acceptable for specific social sectors." "Interdiscourse," in this sense, can be observed in "elementary literary forms ... shared by literary and everyday discourses"—imagery, description, character, and myth—which are the conditions for the broaching and settling of conflicts. Jürgen Link and Wulf Wülfing, eds., *Bewegung und Stillstand in Metaphern und Mythen. Fallstudien zum Verhältnis von elementarem Wissen und Literatur im 19. Jahrhundert* (Stuttgart: Klett-Cotta, 1984), 13, 10, 7 (my translation). For an earlier introduction of this concept, see chapter 3, "Reveries."

21. Raymond Williams, *Culture and Society 1780–1950,* 2nd edition (Harmondsworth: Penguin, 1961), 127. Williams discusses this "traditional idea" in its variants in Coleridge, Mill, Newman, Arnold, and others. The quotation from Coleridge is from *Table Talk,* as given by Williams, 73.

22. J. S. Mill, *Utilitarianism,* in *Utilitarianism, On Liberty, Essay on Bentham,* edited by Mary Warnock (London and Glasgow, 1962), 258.

23. Matthew Arnold, *Culture and Anarchy, The Complete Prose Works of Matthew Arnold,* edited by R. H. Super (Ann Arbor: University of Michigan Press, 1968), 5:215–16.

24. John Ruskin, *Munera Pulveris, The Complete Works of John Ruskin,* edited by E. T. Cook and Alexander Wedderburn (London: Allen, 1905), 17:153; Ruskin, *Fors Clavigera* (Letter 70, Oct. 1876), *The Complete Works,* 28:713.

25. Arnold, *Culture and Anarchy,* 145–46 (my italics). Henry James, *Washington Square,* in *The Bodley Head Henry James,* edited by Leon Edel (London: The Bodley Head, 1967), 203.

26. Mintz, *A Prison of Expectations,* 36, 38 (my italics).

27. The concept "supplement" has been introduced and explicated by Jacques Derrida in his *De la Grammatologie* (Paris: Editions de Minuit, 1967).

28. See chapter 1, "Verse Fables of Satire and Caricature."

29. See chapter 4, "A Glance at the Contemporary Novel," on parabolic insets in Shaw's *An Unsocial Socialist.*

30. See chapter 4, "Aesop in Strange Garb."

31. Margaret Mason Kenda, "Poetic Justice and the Ending Trick in the Victorian Novel," *Genre* 8 (1975): 336.

32. For the formation of, and conflict between, verbal and visual discourses around "Angel in the House" speech in a late Victorian magazine story and the contemporary context of these discourses, see my article "Rivalisierende Diskurse in Text und Bild."

33. For *classic realism* and *closure,* see chapter 5, "Narrator and Narratee," first note.

CONCLUSION

1. R. L. Stevenson, *Works,* XX, following p. 382. Cf. Wendy R. Katz, "'Mark, Printed on the Opposing Page': Robert Louis Stevenson's *Moral Emblems,*" *Emblematica* 2 (1987): 337–54.

Select Bibliography

SOURCES

To facilitate the reader's access to rare items I have added libraries and shelf-marks:

BL = British Library, London

V&A = Victoria and Albert Museum, London

JFK = John F. Kennedy Institute, Free University, Berlin

LCW = Library of Congress, Washington.

Abricht, Johann (i.e., Jonathan Birch). *Divine Emblems.* London: T. Ward, 1838. (*BL* 1164.k.1.)

Adams, William. *Sacred Allegories.* London: Rivingtons, 1855. (*BL* 1509//364.)

Adams, William D., ed. *Songs of Society from Anne to Victoria.* London: Pickering, 1880. (*BL* 11603.cc.10.)

Ade, George. *Fables in Slang.* London and Chicago: Pearson, 1900. (*BL* X.909/6052; 012305.e.23.)

Aesop in Downing Street ... Published under the Superintendence of a Society for the Diffusion of Useful Knowledge. London: Roake & Varty. 1831. (*BL* 1164.d.8.(2).)

Aesop Junior in America: Being a Series of Fables Written Especially for the People of the United States of America. New York: Day, 1834. (*JFK* GA 1000.A.254.)

"Aesop's Fables—Cabinet Edition" (1881). Broadsheet. (*BL* 188.d.3.(112).)

Aesop's Fables. Illustrated by Ernest Griset. With Text Based Chiefly upon Croxall, La Fontaine, and L'Estrange. Revised and Re-Written by J. B. Rundell. London: Cassell, 1869. (*BL* 12305.i.26.)

Aesop's Fables. With Upwards of One Hundred And Fifty Emblematical Devices. London: J. Booker, 1821. (*BL* 12304.a.7.)

Anderdon, W. H. *The Christian Aesop: Ancient Fables Teaching Eternal Truths.* London: Burns, Oates, 1871. (*BL* 12305.bb.21.)

Arnold, Matthew. *The Complete Prose Works of Matthew Arnold,* edited by R. H. Super. Vol. 5. Ann Arbor, Mich.: University of Michigan Press, 1968.

Aveline, E. L. *The Mother's Fables in Verse: Designed, Through the Medium of Amusement, to Correct Some of the Faults and Follies of Children.* London: Darton, Harvey, & Darton, 1812. (*BL* Ch. 810/5; *V&A* 60.M.97.)

Baldwin, Edward (i.e., William Godwin). *Fables Ancient and Modern, Adapted for the Use of Children, from Three to Eight Years of Age.* London: Hodgkins, 1805. (*BL* Ch.800/50.)

Bennett, C. H. *The Fables of Aesop and Others Translated into Human Na-*

ture, Designed and Drawn on the Wood by C. H. Bennett. London: W. Kent, 1857. (*BL* 12305.g.11.)

Bewick, Thomas. *The Works of Thomas Bewick ... Printed for Emerson Charnley ... By S. Hodgson. Vol. 1: Select Fables.* Newcastle: Charnley, 1820. (*V&A* Drawer 117).

————. *Bewick's Select Fables of Aesop and Others ... Faithfully Reprinted From the Rare Newcastle Edition Published by T. Saint in 1784. With ... an Illustrated Preface by Edwin Pearson.* First published 1871. London: Bickers and Son, 1886. (*V&A* G.28.Y.3.)

"Bidpai." *The Fables of Pilpay. Cuts by A. R. Branston.* London: Baldwin, Cradock, & Joy, 1818. (*V&A* Dyce 7469.12.mo.)

————. *The Morall Philosophie of Doni. (Translated) By Sir Thomas North ... Edited and Introduced by Joseph Jacobs.* London: D. Nutt, 1888. (*BL* 12202.ff.1.)

Blake, William. *William Blake's Writings.* Edited by G. E. Bentley, Jr. Vol. 1. Oxford: Clarendon Press, 1978.

The Book of Humorous Poetry. With Illustrations by Charles A. Doyle. Edinburgh: Nimmo, 1867. (*BL* 11602.aaa.4.)

Boothby, Brooke. *Fables and Satires.* Edinburgh: Constable, 1809. (*BL* 11646.eee.46.)

Brady, J. H. *Little Fables For Little Folks.* First published 1835. London: Cassell 1869. (*BL* 12304.bb.40.)

Brett, S. W. *Roman Fables: Cunningly Devised to Support the Arrogant Claims and the Unscriptural Dogmas of the Apostate Roman Church.* London: Thynne, 1898. (*BL* 3939.a.61.)

Brontë, Patrick. *Cottage Poems.* Halifax: Holdren, 1811. (*BL* 11646.ccc.8.)

Brookfield, Olive. *Aesop's Fables for Little Readers. Told by Mrs. Arthur Brookfield.* London: Fisher Unwin, 1888. (*BL* 12305.i.11.)

Browning, Elisabeth B. *The Poetical Works.* London: Frowde, 1904.

Bunyan, John. *A Book for Boys and Girls.* (Published in 1724 as *Divine Emblems or, Temporal Things Spritualized*). In *The Miscellaneous Works of John Bunyan,* edited by Roger Sharrock. Vol. 6. Oxford: Clarendon Press, 1980.

Burns, Robert. *The Poems and Songs of Robert Burns.* Edited by James Kinsley. Vol. 1. Oxford: Clarendon Press, 1968.

Busch, Wilhelm. *Werke.* Edited by Friedrich Bohne. Wiesbaden, Berlin: Vollmer, 1959.

Byrne, J. F. *The Fables of Aesop, and Other Fabulists, in Verse.* London: Printed for the Author, 1835. (*BL* 12304.ccc.35.)

Caldecott, Randolph. *Some of Aesop's Fables with Modern Instances Shewn in Designs by Randolph Caldecott, from New Translations by Alfred Caldecott, M.A.* London: Macmillan, 1883. (*BL* 12304.1.13.)

Carroll, Lewis. *The Annotated Alice.* Edited by Martin Gardner. Harmondsworth: Penguin, 1970.

————. "The Hunting of the Snark." In *The Complete Works of Lewis Carroll.* With an Introduction by Alexander Woolcott. London: Nonesuch Press, 1939.

Carryl, G. W. *Fables for the Frivolous (with Apologies to La Fontaine).* London and New York: Harper & Bros., 1898. (*BL* 12304.i.6.)

Cobbin, Ingram. *Moral Fables and Parables*. London: Westley & Davis, 1832. (*BL* 637.a.37.)

Coleridge, S. T. *The Complete Poetical Works of S. T. Coleridge*. Edited by E. H. Coleridge. Vol. 2I. Oxford: Clarendon Press, 1912.

(Collinson, John). *Fables, Dedicated to Temperance Societies. By a Durham Clergyman*. London: New British Temperance Society, 1840. (*BL* 637.e.42.)

(Corner, Julia). *Familiar Fables: In Easy Language, Suited to the Juvenile Mind, by Miss Corner; the Illustrations by Alfred Crowquill and James Northcote*. London: Dean and Son, 1854. (*BL* 12305.f.16.)

Crane, Walter. *Flora's Feast*. London: Cassell, 1889. (*BL* 11651.1.21.)

———. *Cartoons for the Cause, 1886–1896*. London: The Twentieth Century Press, 1896. Reprint; London: The Journeyman Press, 1976. (*BL* D-1755.a.25.)

——— (and William J. Linton). *The Baby's Own Aesop. Being the Fables Condensed in Rhyme. With Portable Morals Pictorially Pointed out by Walter Crane*. London: Warne, 1887. (*BL* 12811.e.19.)

Crithannah, Job (i.e., Jonathan Birch). *Fifty-one Original Fables, With Morals and Ethical Index ... Embellished with Eighty-Five Original Designs by R. Cruikshank: Engraved on Wood*. London: Hamilton, Adams & Co., 1833. (*BL* 637.g.8.)

Crowquill, Alfred (i.e., Alfred Henry and Charles Robert Forrester). *Picture Fables*. London: Grant & Griffith, 1854. (*BL* 12305.g.2.)

(Croxall, Samuel). *Fables of Aesop and Others: Newly Done into English, With an Application to Each Fable*. London: Tonson & Watts, 1722. (*BL* C.70.c.9.)

Cupples, Anne Jane. *Fables Illustrated by Stories From Real Life*. London: Nelson, 1874. (*BL* 12304.bb.3.)

Darwin, Charles. *On the Origin of Species* (1859). In *The Works of Charles Darwin*. Edited by Paul H. Barrett and R. B. Freeman. London: Pickering, 1988.

Davenport, E. [*sic*], ed. *Story Poems for Young and Old*. London: Cassell, 1891. (*BL* 11602.ee.42.)

Davies, James. *The Fables of Babrius, in Two Parts, Translated into English Verse ... by the Reverend James Davies*. London: Lockwood, 1860. (*BL* 12304.b.37.)

Davis, Mary Anne. *Fables in Verse: From Aesop, La Fontaine, and Others*. London: Harris, 1813; London: Newman, 1822. (*BL* 12305.cc.32. and 12305.bb.13.)

Dene, Edewaerd de. *De warachtighe Fabulen der Dieren*. Brügge: de Clerck, 1567. (*BL* Department of Prints and Drawings)

(Dixon, Sarah). *Fables for Children* (1804). Collected in *The Works of Mrs. Casterton* (i.e., Sarah Dixon). Edited by N. [*sic*] Rogers. 1827 (mostly in MS). (*BL* 1568/857.)

Entertaining Fables for the Instruction of Children. Embellished with Cuts. (In verse.) Derby: Drewry, 1820. (*BL* Ch.800.276.)

Fables and Fancies. London: Maxwell, 1884. (*BL* 1870.c.1.)

Fables and Pictures for the Nursery, Fire Side, and School. London: Edinburgh, and New York: Nelson, 1855. (*BL* 1163.a.38.)

Fables and Poems by T. London: Saunders, Otley, and Co., 1861. (*BL* 11650.aa.44.)

Fables and True Stories of Children. London: Varty, [11]1855. (*BL* 12305.a.26(3).)

Fables for Five Years Old. London: Clowes, 1820. (*BL* 11603.b.40(2).)

Fables for the Nursery. London: Harris, 1824. (*BL* 012305.e.18.)

Fables for the Voters. Colchester: Benham, 1892. (*BL* 1879.c.4.(54).)

Fables in Prose and Verse. London: Burns, 1843. (*BL* 1362..a.25(3).)

Fables in Verse, A Book for the Young. London: Nelson, 1868. (*BL* 12808.aa.4.)

Familiar Fables in Prose and Verse by the Most Eminent Fabulists of All Ages and Countries. Embellished with Engravings after ... Grandville. London: Griffin, 1866. (*BL* 12304.bbb.36.)

Famous Fables in Modern Verse. London and Edinburgh: Nelson, 1865. (*BL* 12304.aaa.17.)

Favourite Fables in Prose and Verse. With ... Illustrations ... by Harrison Weir. London: Griffith and Farran, 1870. (*BL* 12304.ee.28.)

Fitz-Aesop, Francis (pseud.). *Fables of the Day: Written and Arranged for the Artless of All Ages.* London: Maunder, 1831. (*BL* T.1368.(2).)

Froude, J. A. *Short Studies on Great Subjects.* Vol. 1. London: Longman, 1886. (*BL* 12272.i.14.)

Gatty, Margaret. *Parables From Nature.* (Five series. London, [1] 1855–71.) *With a Memoir of the Author by Her Daughter Juliana H. Ewing.* London: Bell, 1880. (*BL* 12809.m.7.)

Gay, John. *Fables ... with Memoir, Introduction, and Annotations, by Octavius Freire Owen ... With Drawings by William Harvey, Engraved by the Brothers Dalziel.* London: Routledge, 1854.

Gilder, J. L., ed., *Representative Poems of Living Poets. American and English. Selected by the Poets Themselves.* Introduced by G. P. Lathrup. London: Cassell, 1886. (*BL* 11601.i.16.)

Godolphin, Mary (i.e., Lucy Aikin). *Aesop's Fables in Words of One Syllable ... Printed in the Learners' Style of Phonography ... by Isaac Pitman.* 1891. (*BL* 12991.b.50.(13.)

Gow, Gregson. *New Light Through Old Windows. A Series of Stories Illustrating Fables of Aesop.* London: Blackie, 1883. (*BL* 12810.c.16.)

Griset, Ernest, See *Aesop's Fables.*

Gurney, Richard. *Fables on Men and Manners.* London: Davison, 1809. (*BL* 12305.cc.21).

Hardy, Thomas. *The Complete Poetical Works of Thomas Hardy.* Edited by Samuel Hynes. Vol. 1. Oxford: Oxford University Press, 1982.

Henryson, Robert. *The Poems and Fables of Robert Henryson, Now First Collected With Notes and a Memoir of His Life by D. Laing.* Edinburgh: W. Paterson, 1865. (*V&A* Dyce 4630.M.8vo.)

Hey, Wilhelm. *Picture Fables. Drawn by Otto Speckter, Engraved by the Brothers Dalziel.* Translated by H. W. Dulcken. London: Routledge, 1858. (*BL* 12305.d.13.)

Hogarth Illustrated. Edited by John Ireland. 2nd edition. Vol. 1. London: Boydell, 1804.

Instructive Fables for Christian Scholars. By the Author of "The Last Day of the Week" (i.e., Eliza Cheap). London: Seeley, 1834. (*BL* 12304.aa.60.)

Jackson, Lewis, ed. *Fables de Florian, with Explanations of the Difficult Words ... New Edition.* London: 1837. (*BL* 1507/1230.)

————. ed. *Jean Pierre Florian's Fables.* London: Law, 1851.

James, Thomas. *Aesop's Fables: A New Version, Chiefly From Original Sources ... With ... Illustrations Designed by John Tenniel.* London: Murray, 1848. (*BL* 12305.e.32.)

Kelly, Arthur. *The Rosebud and Other Tales. Pictured by Walter Crane.* London: Fisher Unwin, 1909. (*BL* 12804.y.20.)

(Krylov. I. A.). *Krilof and His Fables, Translated by W. R. S. Ralston.* London: Strahan, 1869. (*V&A* 55.D.3.)

La Fontaine, Jean de. *Œuvres complètes.* Edited by René Groos and Jacques Schiffrin. Vol. 1. Paris: Gallimard 1954.

Le Gros, W. B. *Fables and Tales, Suggested by the Frescos of Pompeii and Herculaneum.* Twenty Engraved Plates by F. Bromley. London: R. Bentley, 1835. (*BL* 637.g.9.; *V&A* 29.R.5.)

L'Estrange, Roger. *Fables of Aesop ... With Morals and Reflexions.* Vol. 1. London: Sare, 1692. Vol. 2. London: Sare, 1699. (*BL* Ch. 690/2; 12304.i.11.)

The Leisure Hour. A Family Journal of Instruction and Recreation. No. 775 (November 1866). (*BL* P.P.60004.1.)

(Linton, W. J.). *The Wisdom of Aesop, Condensed: Fables in Familiar Verse, with Delightfully Short Morals, for the Use and Amusement of Rail-road Travelers and Others, by P. J.* (Hamden, Conn.): A.P.P. (i.e., Appledore Private Press), 1880. (*V&A* 95.W.Box I.)

Lytton, Edward Robert Bulwer, earl of. *Fables in Song.* 2 vols. ([1] Edinburgh: Blackwood, 1874, *BL* 1304.e.13.) [2]Leipzig: Tauchnitz, 1874.

Mannich, Johann. *Sacra Emblemata LXXVI in quibus summa uniuscuiusque evangeli rotunde adumbratur.* Nürnberg, 1625. (*BL* 636.g.22.(1.))

Miles, A. H., ed. *The Poets and the Poetry of the Nineteenth Century.* Vols. 5, 6. London, 1905. Vol. 10. London: Routledge, 1907. (*BL* 11604.d.1.)

Mrs. T. (i.e., Trimmer, Sarah). *The Ladder to Learning: a Collection of Fables, Arranged Progressively in Words of One, Two, and Three Syllables, With Original Morals, Edited and Improved by Mrs. T.* 16th edition. London: Harris, 1841. (*V&A* 60.F.61.)

Molesworth, Mary Louisa (i.e., Agnes de Havilland). *The Children of the Castle.* London: Macmillan, 1890. (*BL* 12811.c.37.)

Northcote, James. *One Hundred Fables, Original and Selected. Embellished with Two Hundred and Eighty Engravings on Wood.* London: Lawford, 1828. (*BL* 831.i.21. *V&A* 29.S.9.)

————. *The Artist's Book of Fables, Illustrated by 280 Engravings ... After Designs by the Late James Northcote.* London: Bohn, 1845. (*BL* 12304.ee.27.)

————. *Fables, Original and Selected, by James Northcote, R.A.* London: Routledge, 1857. (*BL* 12304.d.26.)

————. See also Corner, Julia.

Pacis, Oliver. *Temperance Rays From Aesop's Lamp.* London: Kelly, 1900. (*BL* 8436.c.30.)

Paton, F. N., ed. *Bards and the Birds*. London: Reeves & Turner, 1894. (*BL* 11601.ee.39.)

Peacock, Thomas Love. *Crotchet Castle*. In *The Novels of Thomas Love Peacock*. Edited by David Garnett. London: Hart-Davis, 1948.

Perring, Philip. *The Fables of Florian, Done into English Verse*. London: Longman, 1896. (*BL* 12305.dd.22.)

The Queen's London. A Pictorial and Descriptive Record of the Streets, Buildings, Parks, and Scenery of the Great Metropolis. London: Cassell, 1896.

(Sandham, Elizabeth, ed.). *Claris de Florian. Select Fables. Written for the Purpose of Instilling in the Minds of Early Youth a True Sense of Religion and Virtue. Translated ... by the Author of "A Cup of Sweets."* London: Harris, 1806. (*BL* 1490.p.2.)

———. *The Perambulations of a Bee and a Butterfly, in Which are Delineated Those Smaller Traits of Character Which Escape the Observation of Larger Spectators*. London: Lewis, 1812. (*BL* CH.810.166.)

Schanz, Pauline. *101 neue Fabeln*. Berlin, 1888.

Sewell, Anna. *Black Beauty: His Grooms and Companions. The Autobiography of a Horse*. First published 1877. Harmondsworth: Penguin, 1954.

(Sharpe, R. S.). *Old Friends in a New Dress; or, Familiar Fables in Verse*. London: Harvey & Darton, 1820. (*V&A* 60 R. Box VI.)

Shaw, George Bernard. *An Unsocial Socialist* ([1]1884). London: Virago, 1980.

Shelley, Percy B. *Poetical Works*. Edited by Thomas Hutchinson. 2nd edition. London: Oxford University Press, 1970.

Steers, H. [*sic*]. *Aesop's Fables, New Versified from the Best English Editions*. Hull: Printed for the Author, 1803. (*BL* 637.i.10.)

Stephens, H. L. *The Fables of Aesop*. New York: Scribner, 1868. (*V&A* 95.T.44.)

Stevenson, Robert Louis. *Works*. Pentland Edition. Edited by Edmund Gosse. Vol. 20. London: Cassell, 1907.

(Taylor, Jane and Anne). *Original Poems for Infant Minds. By Several Young Persons*. London, 1805. (*BL* C.117.a.58.)

Taylor, Jefferys. *Aesop in Rhyme*. London: Baldwin, Cradock and Joy, 1823. (*BL* 012305.e.61.)

Townsend. G. F. *Fables of Aesop, with New Applications, Morals, etc.* Illustrated by Harrison Weir. London: Warne, 1866. (*BL* 12304.bbb.35)

Wallbridge, Arthur (i.e., W. A. B. Lunn). *Bizarre Fables*. London: Orr, 1842. (*BL* 1163.b.1.)

Watts, Isaac. *Divine Songs Attempted in Easy Language for the Use of Children*. First edition 1715. In *The Works of the English Poets*. Edited by Alexander Chalmers. Vol. 2. London: J. Johnson and others, 1810.

Weir, Harrison. *Three Hundred Aesop's Fables*. London: Routledge, 1867. (*BL* 12304.bbb.33)

———. See also Townsend.

Whitney, Geffrey. *A Choice of Emblemes*. First published Leyden, 1585. Edited by Henry Green. New York: Blom, Benjamin, 1967.

Wills, W. H., ed. *Poets' Wit and Humour*. London: Bell & Daldy, 1860. (*BL* 1347.g.19.)

Wordsworth, William. *The Poetical Works.* Edited by Ernest de Selincourt. Vol. 2. Oxford: Clarendon Press, ² 1952.

Yeld, Charles, ed., *Florian's Fables. Selected and Edited ... by the Rev. Charles Yeld ... with Philological and Explanatory Notes.* London: Macmillan, 1888, 1897, 1905. (*BL* 12200.eee.1/1.)

CRITICISM

Altick, R. D. *Victorian People and Ideas.* London: Dent, 1973.

Arnold, Matthew. *Culture and Anarchy.* In *The Complete Prose Works of Matthew Arnold.* Edited by R. H. Super, Vol. 5. Ann Arbor: University of Michigan Press, 1965.

Auerbach, Nina, and U. C. Knoepflmacher. *Forbidden Journeys: Fairy Tales and Fantasies by Victorian Women Writers.* Chicago, London: University of Chicago Press, 1992.

Bär, Eugen. "The Language of the Unconscious According to Jacques Lacan." *Semiotica* 3 (1971): 241–68.

Bakhtin, Mikhail. *The Dialogical Principle.* Edited by Tzvetan Todorov. Translated by Wlad Godzich. Theory and History of Literature 13. Manchester: Manchester University Press, 1984.

Bausinger, Hermann. "Die moralischen Tiere." *Universitas* 45 (1990): 241–51.

Beaver, Patrick. *The Spice of Life. Pleasures of the Victorian Age.* London: Elm Tree Books, 1979.

Belsey, Catherine. *Critical Practice.* London: Methuen, 1980.

Bentley, Nicolas. *The Victorian Scene.* London: Weidenfeld & Nicolson, 1968.

Bibby, Cyril. *The Art of the Limerick.* London: Research Publishing, 1978.

Blackham, H. J. *The Fable as Literature.* London: Athlone Press, 1985.

Bode, Christoph. *Ästhetik der Ambiguität. Zur Funktion und Bedeutung von Mehrdeutigkeit in der Literatur der Moderne.* Tübingen: Niemeyer, 1988.

Burpee, L. J. "Literary Piracy." *Queen's Quarterly* 46 (1939): 295–303.

Bush, Douglas. *Mythology and the Romantic Tradition in English Poetry.* New York, Cambridge: Harvard University Press, 1937.

Bush, Geoffrey. "Songs." In *Music in Britain: The Romantic Age 1800–1914.* Edited by Nicholas Temperley. London: Athlone, 1981.

Carnes, Pack. *Fable Scholarship, An Annotated Bibliography.* New York: Garland, 1985.

Chitty, Susan. *The Woman Who Wrote Black Beauty: Anna Sewell.* London: Hodder, 1971.

Coenen, Hans Georg. "Zur Deutbarkeit von Fabeln." *Linguistische Berichte* 4 (1976): 15–21.

Cole, G. D. H. *A Short History of the British Working Class Movement.* 2nd edition. London: Allen & Unwin, 1948.

Coward, Rosalind, and John Ellis. *Language and Materialism: Developments in Semiology and the Theory of the Subject.* London: Routledge & Kegan Paul, 1977.

Crane, Walter. *An Artist's Reminiscences.* London: Methuen, 1907.

Cruse, Amy. *The Englishman and His Books.* London: Harrap, 1930.

————. *The Victorians and Their Books*. London: Allen & Unwin, 1935.

Dale, Peter A. "George Eliot's 'Brother Jacob': Fables and the Physiology of Common Life." *Philological Quarterly* 64 (1985): 17–35.

Daniel, S. H. "Political and Philosophical Uses of Fables in Eighteenth-Century England." *The Eighteenth Century: Theory and Interpretation* 23 (1982): 151–71.

Davis, R. C. *Lacan and Narration. The Psychoanalytic Difference in Narrative Theory*. Baltimore: Johns Hopkins, 1984.

Delgado, Alan. *Victorian Entertainment*. Newton Abbot, England: David & Charles, 1971.

Derrida, Jacques. *De la Grammatologie*. Paris: Editions de Minuit, 1967.

Dithmar, Reinhardt. *Die Fabel. Geschichte, Struktur, Didaktik*. Paderborn: Schöningh, [7]1988.

Doderer, Klaus. *Fabeln. Formen, Figuren, Lehren*. München: dtv, 1977.

Dölvers, Horst. *Der Erzähler Robert Louis Stevenson*. Berne: Francke, 1969.

————. "Gegen die Despotie der Fakten. Walter Cranes Bilderbuchphantasien zwischen Neorenaissance und Art Nouveau." In *Englische Buchillustration im europäischen Kontext. Katalog zur Ausstellung der TU Berlin, 12.12.1989–12.1.1990*. Edited by Joachim Möller, 41–55. Berlin: Technische Universität, 1989.

————. "Depiction vs. Picturing. Subversive Illustrations in a Victorian Picture-Book." *Word and Image* 7 (1991): 201–22.

————. "'Fables Less and Less Fabulous.' The English Verse Fable in the Nineteenth Century." *Anglia* 111 (1993): 373–409.

————. "'Quite a Serious Division of Creative Literature'. Lord Lytton's *Fables in Song* and R. L. Stevenson's Prose Fables." *Archiv für das Studium der neueren Sprachen und Literaturen* 230 (1993): 62–77.

————. "'Let Beasts Bear Gentle Minds.' Variety and Conflict of Discourses in Anna Sewell's *Black Beauty*." *Arbeiten aus Anglistik und Amerikanistik* 18 (1993): 195–215.

————. *Walter Cranes Aesop im Kontext seiner Entstehung. Buchkunst und Bilderbuch im viktorianischen England*. Kassel: Edition Reichenberger, 1994.

Drabble, Margaret (ed.). *The Oxford Companion to English Literature*. 5th edition. Oxford: Oxford University Press, 1985.

Easthope, Antony. *Poetry as Discourse*. London: Methuen, 1983.

————. *Poetry and Phantasy*. Cambridge: Cambridge University Press, 1989.

Elm, Theo. *Die moderne Parabel*. UTB 1630. München: Fink, 1991.

————, and Peter Hasubek, eds. *Fabel und Parabel. Kulturgeschichtliche Prozesse im achtzehnten Jahrhundert*. München: Fink, 1994.

Engen, R. K. *Walter Crane as a Book Illustrator*. London: St. Martin's Press, 1975.

Floud, R. C., and D. McCloskey, eds. *The Economic History of Britain Since 1700*. Vol. 2. Cambridge, London, etc.: Cambridge University Press, 1981.

Foucault, Michel. "The Discourse on Language." ([1] 1970). In *The Archeology of Knowledge*. London: Tavistock Publications, 1972.

Foucault, Michel. *Power/Discourse. Selected Interviews and Other Writings.* Edited by Colin Gordon. Brighton, Sussex: Harvester Press, 1980.

Furness, J. C. *Voyage to Windward. The Life of R. L. Stevenson.* London: Faber, 1952.

Genette, Gérard. *Palimpsestes—La Littérature au second degré.* Paris: Editions du seuil, 1982.

Gittings, R., and J. Manton. *Claire Clairmont and the Shelleys 1789—1879.* Oxford: Oxford University Press, 1992.

Gohrbandt, Detlev. "Zur Semantik und Didaktik der Fabel: Bild und Text bei James Northcote und Randolph Caldecott." *Die neueren Sprachen* 91 (1992): 598–614.

Grubmüller, Klaus. "Semantik der Fabel." In *Third International Beast Epic, Fable, and Fabliau Colloquium, Münster 1979.* Edited by Jan Goossens and Timothy Sodmann, 111–34. Cologne: Böhlau, 1981.

————. "Fabel, Exempel, Allegorese. Über Sinnbildungsverfahren und Verwendungszusammenhänge." In *Exempel und Exempelsammlungen.* Edited by Walter Haug and Burghart Wachinger, 58–76. Tübingen: Niemeyer, 1991.

Grzybek, Peter. "Invariant Meaning Structures in Texts: Proverb and Fable." In *Issues in Slavic Literary and Cultural Theory.* Edited by Karl Eimermacher, Peter Grzybek, and Georg Witte, 349–89. Bochum: Brockmeyer, 1989.

Guter, Josef. "Fünfhundert Jahre Fabelillustration." *Das Antiquariat* 22 (1972): 25–31, 41–47, 89–93.

Haass, Sabine. *Gedichtanthologien der viktorianischen Zeit. Eine Buchgeschichtliche Untersuchung zum Wandel des literarischen Geschmacks.* Nürnberg: Carl, 1986.

Harlan, A. B. *Owen Meredith. A Critical Biography of Robert, First Earl of Lytton.* New York: Columbia University Press, 1946.

Harris, W. V. *Dictionary of Concepts in Literary Criticism and Theory.* Reference Sources for the Social Sciences and Humanities 12. New York, London: Greenwood Press, 1992.

Hassauer, Friederike. *Die Philosophie der Fabeltiere.* München: Fink, 1986.

Hasubek, Peter. *Die Fabel. Theorie, Geschichte und Rezeption einer Gattung.* Berlin: Schmidt, 1982.

————, ed. *Fabelforschung.* Darmstadt: Wissenschaftliche Buchgesellschaft, 1983.

Hearn, M. P. "Nursery Aesthetics: Walter Crane and His Picture Books for Children." *American Book Collector,* N.S., 2 no. 4 (1981): 2–12; 2 no. 5 (1981): 19–33.

Henderson, A. C. "Medieval Beasts and Modern Cages: The Making of Meaning in Fables and Bestiaries." *PMLA* 97 (1982): 40–49.

Henkel, Arthur, and Albrecht Schöne, eds. *Emblemata. Handbuch zur Sinnbildkunst des 16. und 17. Jahrhunderts.* Stuttgart: Metzler, 1967.

Hermerén, Göran. "Two Concepts of Illustration." In *Representation and Meaning in the Visual Arts,* 55–76. Copenhagen: Scandinavian University Books, 1969.

Heydebrand, Renate v. "Parabel, Geschichte eines Begriffs zwischen Rhetorik, Poetik und Hermeneutik." *Archiv für Begriffsgeschichte,* 34 (1991): 27–122.

Hobbs, Anne S., ed. *Fables*. London: Victoria & Albert Museum, 1986.

Hodnett, Edward. *Aesop in England. The Transmission of Motifs in Seventeenth Century Illustrations of Aesop's Fables*. Charlottesville, Va.: University Press of Virginia, 1979.

———. *Francis Barlow, First Master of English Book Illustration*. London, Scholar Press, 1978.

Hönnighausen, Lothar. *Präraphaeliten und Fin de Siècle. Symbolistische Tendenzen in der englischen Spätromantik*. München: Fink, 1971.

Holloway, John, and Joan Black. *Later English Broadside Ballads*. Vol. 2. London: Routledge & Kegan Paul, 1979.

Houfe, Simon. *The Dictionary of British Book Illustrators and Caricaturists*. Woodbridge, Suff.: Antique Collectors' Club, 1978.

Hueck, Monika. *Textstruktur und Gattungssystem. Studien zum Verhältnis vom Emblem und Fabel im 16. und 17. Jahrhundert*. Kronberg/T.: Scriptor, 1975.

Huete, S. B. "John Gay's Fables I and II: A Study in the 18th Century Fable." University of S. Miss. Dissertation, 1973.

Jacobs, Arthur. "The British Isles." In *A History of Song*. Edited by Denis Stevens and others. 124–93. London: Hutchinson, 1960.

James, Henry. *The Bodley Head Henry James*. Edited by Leon Edel. London: The Bodley Head, 1967.

Jolles, André. *Einfache Formen* (First published 1930). 4th edition. Tübingen: Niemeyer, 1968.

Kenda, Margaret Mason. "Poetic Justice and the Ending Trick in the Victorian Novel." *Genre* 8 (1975): 336–51.

Katz, Wendy R. "'Mark, Printed on the Opposing Page': Robert Louis Stevenson's *Moral Emblems*." *Emblematica* 2 (1987): 337–54.

Knauth, K. A. "Fabula Rasa." In *Das fremde Wort*. Festschrift für Karl Maurer. Edited by Ilse Nolting-Hauff and Joachim Schulze, 51 – 80. Amsterdam: B. R. Grüner, 1988.

Lacan, Jacques. *Ecrits*. Paris: Editions du seuil, 1966.

———. *Le Seminaire de Jacques Lacan*. Texte établi par Jacques-Alain Miller. Vol. 2. Paris: Editions du seuil, 1978.

———. "The Mirror-Phase as Formative of the Function of the I." *New Left Review* 51 (1968): 71–77.

———. *Le Discours de Rome* (1953). Edited and translated by Anthony Wilden. In Wilden, Anthony. *The Language of the Self. The Function of Language in Psychoanalysis*. Baltimore: Johns Hopkins Press, 1968.

Lattimore, C. R. *English Nineteenth-Century Press-Moulded Glass*. London: Barrie & Jenkins, 1979.

Leibfried, Erwin. *Fabel*. Stuttgart: Metzler, ⁴ 1982.

Lindner, Hermann. *Fabeln der Neuzeit: England, Frankreich und Deutschland. Ein Lese-und Arbeitsbuch*. Munich: Fink, 1978.

Link, Jürgen, and Wulf Wülfing, eds. *Bewegung und Stillstand in Metaphern und Mythen. Fallstudien zum Verhältnis von elementarem Wissen und Literatur im 19. Jahrhundert*. Stuttgart: Klett-Cotta, 1984.

Linton, William J. *The Masters of Wood Engraving*. London: Stevens, 1889.

———. *Memories.* London: Lawrence & Bullen, 1895.

MacCabe, Colin. *James Joyce and the Revolution of the Word.* London: Macmillan, 1978.

Macdonell, Diane. *Theories of Discourse, An Introduction.* Oxford: Blackwell, 1986.

McGovern, Barbara. "Pier Glasses and Sympathy in Eliot's *Middlemarch.*" *Victorian Newsletter* 72 (1987): 6–8.

McKendry, J. J. *Aesop. Five Centuries of Illustrated Fables.* New York: Metropolitan Museum of Art, 1964.

Meller, Horst. *Zum Verstehen englischer Gedichte.* Munich: Fink, 1985.

Metz, Nancy A. "Ayala's Angel: Trollope's Late Fable of Change and Choice." In *Dickens Studies Annual: Essays on Victorian Fiction* 9 (1981): 217–32.

Mill, John Stuart. *Utilitarianism.* In *Utilitarianism, On Liberty, Essay on Bentham.* Edited by Mary Warnock. London and Glasgow: Collins, 1962.

Miller, J. Hillis. "Sketches by Boz, Oliver Twist, and Cruikshank's Illustrations." In *Charles Dickens and George Cruikshank.* Edited by Ada Nisbet. Los Angeles: University of California Press, 1971.

———. "The Search for Grounds in Literary Study." In *Rhetoric and Form. Deconstruction at Yale.* Edited by R. Con Davis and Ronald Schleifer. Norman: University of Oklahoma Press, 1985.

———. *The Linguistic Moment. From Wordsworth to Stevens.* Princeton N.J.: Princeton University Press, 1985.

———. "'Hieroglyphical Truth' in *Sartor Resartus:* Carlyle and the Language of Parable." In *Victorian Perspectives: Six Essays.* Edited by John Clubbe and Jerome Meckier, 1–20. Newark: University of Delaware Press, 1989.

Mintz, Stephen. *A Prison of Expectations. The Family in Victorian Culture.* New York, London: New York University Press, 1983.

Möller, Joachim. *Romankritik in Großbritannien 1800–1860. Mit einem Kapitel zum Kritikpotential der Illustration.* Anglistische Forschungen 212. Heidelberg: Winter, 1991.

Muir, Percy. *English Children's Books 1600 to 1900.* London: Batsford, 1954.

Needler, Howard. "The Animal Fable among Other Medieval Literary Genres." *New Literary History* 22 (1991): 423–39.

Nerlich, Michael. *Ideology of Adventure. Studies in Modern Consciousness 1100–1750.* Minneapolis, Minn.: University of Minneapolis Press, 1987.

Noakes, Vivien. *Edward Lear, 1812–1888.* Royal Academy of Arts Catalogue. London: Weidenfeld & Nicholson, 1985.

Noel, Thomas. *Theories of the Fable in the Eighteenth Century.* New York and London: Columbia University Press, 1975.

Orel, Harold. *The Victorian Short Story. Development and Triumph of a Literary Genre.* Cambridge: Cambridge University Press, 1986.

Padel, Ruth. "Saddled With Ginger. Women, Men, and Horses." *Encounter* 55 (1980): 47–54.

Patterson, Annabel. *Fables of Power. Aesopian Writing and Political History.* Durham, N.C., and London: Duke University Press, 1991.

Pêcheux, Michel. *Language, Semantics and Ideology: Stating the Obvious* (1st edition 1975). 2nd edition. London: Macmillan, 1982.

Peppin, Brigid and Lucy Micklethwait. *Dictionary of British Book Illustrators, The Twentieth Century.* London: Murray, 1983.

Plessow, Max. *Geschichte der Fabeldichtung in England.* Berlin: Mayer & Müller, 1906.

Posner, Roland. "What Is Culture? Toward a Semiotic Explication of Anthropological Concepts." In *The Nature of Culture.* Edited by Walter A. Koch, 240–95. Bochum: Brockmeyer, 1989.

Quayle, Eric. *The Collector's Book of Children's Books.* London: Studio Vista, 1971.

Quinnam, Barbara. *Fables from Incunabula to Modern Picture Books. A Selective Bibliography.* Washington: Library of Congress, 1966.

Rabkin, Norman. *Shakespeare and the Problem of Meaning.* Chicago: University of Chicago Press, 1981.

Raymond, E. N. *Victorian Viceroy. The Life of Robert, the First Earl of Lytton.* London: Regency Press, 1980.

Reading, Peter. "Equine Feminism." *TLS,* no. 4301 (1985): 975.

Ritvo, Harriet. "Animal Pleasures: Popular Zoology in Eighteenth- and Nineteenth-Century England." *Harvard Library Bulletin* 33 (1985): 239–79.

———. "Learning From Animals: Nature History for Children in the Eighteenth and Nineteenth Centuries." *Children's Literature* 13 (1985): 72–93.

———. *The Animal Estate. The English and Other Creatures in the Victorian Age.* Cambridge: Harvard University Press, 1987.

Rorty, Richard. *Contingency, Irony, and Solidarity.* Cambridge: Cambridge University Press, 1989.

Ruskin, John. *Munera Pulveris.* In *The Complete Works of John Ruskin.* Library Edition. Edited by E. T. Cook and Alexander Wedderburn. Vols. 17, 28. London: Allen, 1905.

Schöne, Albrecht. "Emblemata. Versuch einer Einführung." *DVjS* 37 (1963): 197–231.

———. *Emblematik und Drama im Zeitalter des Barocks.* München: Beck, ²1968.

Scholes, Robert E. *The Fabulators.* New York and Oxford: Oxford University Press, 1967.

Schwarcz, J. H. *Ways of the Illustrator. Visual Communication in Children's Literature.* Chicago: American Library Association, 1982.

Shaw, Valerie. *The Short Story: A Critical Introduction.* London: Longman, 1983.

Shepherd, Gillian. "The Kailyard." In *The History of Scottish Literature.* Edited by Douglas Gifford, 309–20. Vol. 3: The Nineteenth Century. Aberdeen: Aberdeen University Press, 1988.

Sills, R. M. "W. J. Linton at Yale—The Appledore Private Press." *Yale University Library Gazette,* 12 (1938), item 7.

Silverman, Kaja. *The Subject of Semiotics.* New York and Oxford: Oxford University Press, 1983.

Slack, Raymond. *English Pressed Glass 1830–1900.* London: Barrie & Jenkins, 1987.

Smith, F. B. *Radical Artisan. W. J. Linton 1812–1897.* Manchester: Manchester University Press, 1973.

Smith, Greg, and Sarah Hyde (eds.). *Walter Crane 1845–1915. Artist, Designer and Socialist.* London: Lund Humphries and Manchester: The Whitworth Art Gallery, 1989.

Smith, M. E. "The Fable and Kindred Forms." *Journal of English and Germanic Philology* 14 (1915): 519–29.

———. "Notes on the Rimed Fable." *Modern Language Notes* 31 (1916): 206–16.

———. "The Fable as Poetry." *Modern Language Notes* 32 (1917): 466–70.

Spencer, Isobel. *Walter Crane.* London: Vista, 1975.

Stevens, Denis, ed. *A History of Song.* London: Hutchinson, 1960.

Taylor, Gary. *Reinventing Shakespeare: A Cultural History from the Restoration to the Present.* London: Oxford University Press, 1989.

Tiemann, Barbara. *Fabel und Emblem. Gilles Corrozet und die französische Renaissance-Fabel.* München: Fink, 1974.

Tiemann, Hermann. "Wort und Bild in der Fabeltradition bis zu La Fontaine." In *Buch und Welt, Festschrift for Gustav Hofmann.* Edited by Hans Striedl and others, 237–60. Wiesbaden: Harrassowitz, 1965.

Trickett, Rachel. "Cowper, Wordsworth, and the Animal Fable." *Review of English Studies* 34 (1983): 471–80.

Tung, Mason, "Fables in Emblems." *Studies in Iconography* 12 (1988): 43–60.

Verch, Maria. *Das englische Gedicht für Kinder vom 17. bis 20. Jahrhundert. Typen, Themen, Motive.* Heidelberg: Winter, 1983.

Vicinus, Martha. *The Industrial Muse. A Study of Nineteenth-Century Working Class Literature.* London: Croom Helm, 1974.

Vindt, Lidija "Die Fabel als literarisches Genre," *Poetica* 9 (1977): 98–122.

Weinrich, Harald. "Wenn Ihr die Fabel vertreibt." In *Information und Imagination.* Edited by the Bayerische Akademie der Wissenschaften, 61–83. Müchen: Piper, 1973.

Williams, Raymond. *Culture and Society 1780–1950.* 2nd edition. Harmondsworth: Penguin, 1961.

Wilson, A. C. "To Instruct and to Amuse: Some Victorian Views of Aesop's Fables." *Children's Literature Association Quarterly* 9 (1984): 66–68.

Wilson, Harris W., and Diane Long Hoeveler. *English Prose and Criticism in the Nineteenth Century. A Guide to Information Sources.* Detroit: Gale Research, 1979.

Wordsworth, William. *The Prose Works.* Edited by W. J. B. Owen and J. W. Smyser. Vol. 1. Oxford: Clarendon Press, 1974.

General Index

Index of Fables and Fable Collections